D 21

THE LABOUR UNREST

THE
LABOUR UNREST

WHAT IT IS AND
WHAT IT PORTENDS

BY

FRED HENDERSON

Author of " The Case for Socialism," etc.

LONDON
JARROLD & SONS, WARWICK LANE, E.C.

CONTENTS

THE LABOUR UNREST

CHAPTER I

INTRODUCTORY

LOOKING back upon any great period of decisive change in history, we are apt to fall into an illusion of thinking, because we can survey it comprehensively, note its beginnings, follow its development, trace its consequences in the altered outlooks and institutions of the race, and see its significance in relation to the periods before and after, that the men of the time saw it with a comprehension like our own. We picture such periods of great change as being spectacular to the folk taking part in them ; the orderly unfolding of a set drama, scene by scene in the deliberate sequence of the intention of the age. The changes which we see to have actually come about in the course of history we figure to ourselves as ends deliberately aimed at, shaped by the people of the period as builders shape their building to drawn plans. We think of them advancing

B

to a foreseen and calculated emancipation,
advancing in the clear light of day, with all
the incidents and episodes falling purposefully
into their places in an ordered march leading
up to the complete attainment.

Nothing could be further from the truth.
The significance of its own doings and hap-
penings is for the most part hidden from each
generation. Turn from the survey of past
periods to a contemplation of our own current
events, our confusions and doubtful experiments and uncertainties, and the empirical
character of each generation's knowledge of
its own affairs, and of how it will figure in
history when seen in perspective, will be at
once clear to you. For the vast majority of
men nothing ever happens beyond the little
daily inconsequences ; and, as has been truly
said, even in the midst of Armageddon very
few people are aware of anything going on of
greater import than a little more confusion
and muddle than usual round about them.
We move on through Time with a wall of
darkness at our faces ; and the next step is
always into it, a step into mysteries and
uncertainties. Those incidents of a period
which, seen in historic perspective, stand out
in unmistakable significance as index facts
revealing the purpose and character of the

age as an age of historic change, are noted at the time as only trivial incidents in the daily routine, and seen only in disconnected fragments as part of the ordinary confusion of current events.

This contemporary blindness to the obvious signs of impending change is always a marvel to later generations. It seems incredible that the plain direction of the stream of events should go undiscerned. The signs are so obvious, the indications so clear and unmistakable. But before passing judgment of dullness and stupidity upon those who lived in such former periods, it is, I repeat, worth while asking whether we, in our turn, show any more clear-sightedness in reading the obvious signs of our own times than they did in theirs. We can see their completed period as it lies in the clear light of history ; but we see our own period as they saw theirs, full of the confusion of half-done and fragmentary things, of cross purposes and conflicting interests, with a thousand by-ways turning and diverging in all directions, indistinguishable at the moment from what will be seen later on to be the main road of our age's movement in history. If the signs preceding earlier periods of change seem to us to be so very obvious that only a generation of dullards could have failed to recognize them, we must remember that we see them in the full light of their realization in history, an illumination denied to contemporaries. The past is mapped and charted for us ; but the present is always at the cross roads, exploring new country in the dark.

We create our own darkness very largely by our mood of incredulous refusal to look for signs of change at all. The tremendous hold of an established order of things upon the mind of a community blinds the mass of men to any prognostication of things beyond that order. It appears to be one of the laws of human life that no community ever looks for fundamental change in its established order, or even believes such change to be possible or credible. However obvious the signs of such impending change may be, they must, before they can be seen for what they are, break through that absolute reliance upon the stability of the existing order which limits each generation in the interpretation of current events. The signs seem obvious and unmistakable to us in later generations, not only because we see them in the full light of their realization in history, but because we have become accustomed to the changed outlooks and institutions. Take, for example, the great industrial revolution brought about by the machine industry. If you could have depicted the England of to-day to the generation which lived from two hundred to a hundred and fifty years ago, the picture would have been received with scoffing and derision as the nightmare of a maniac. It was a generation mainly agricultural. The great industrial towns had not begun to be. Its industry was handicraft industry, and its tools simple tools capable of personal and individual use, owned by the worker himself. It knew nothing of capitalist and proletariat as we know them to-day. The story of our herded modern town populations, our gigantic machines, and the fundamental changes in social organization brought about by the severance of the producer from control over his own tools and his own labour, and his transformation into a " hand " in a modern factory, would have seemed the most grotesque and incredible thing to them. And yet the signs of it were there, could men but have seen their full significance. We know to-day what it meant in the social and industrial revolution in English life that Kaye should have invented the fly-shuttle in 1750 and Hargreaves the spinning-jenny a few years later. There was a new era, a new form of social organization, deep-reaching change in habits and outlooks and human relationships, perceptible to all men to-day in these beginnings of the machine industry. We not only see them, I repeat, in their full realization in history, but we have become accustomed to the changed outlooks and institutions. The new order is now the old-established order for us, the familiar normal face of the world. It seems eminently reasonable to us that events should have led up to it. Life is reconciled and adjusted to it by use and wont ; it is in the nature of things that it should be just what it is. It holds our mind and imagination in its grip, and limits our interpretation of current affairs to an interpretation within itself, as every established order has always held and limited men's minds ; casting its spell forward so that any future fundamental change in it seems incredible to us, and backward so that all former changes and movements seem to us to have been only the obvious preparatory steps towards it, seen and recognized as such by the men of those earlier days. They no more saw their period in that relation to impending change than we see ours in a similar preparatory and embryonic relation to the future. Theirs, too, was a final, settled, irrevocable order, capable perhaps of modification and betterment in detail, but of nothing so impractical and absurd as revolution in fundamental things ; and they failed to read the signs of their time, which now seem so obvious to us, because the very idea of fundamental change was grotesque and unthinkable to them. Such an interpretation of the significance of current events is always unthinkable to the mass of men—the very last interpretation likely to occur to them, even when it begins to bludgeon an understanding of itself into them with realized facts—because it involves a threat against that established order within which the imagination of each generation is confined.

The signs of impending change were never more obvious than they are to-day. We are far past the stage of subtle and small beginnings. The bludgeoning has commenced. And the general refusal to look beyond the established order of things for interpretation of the signs, the general incapacity even to think of them as signs of change at all, or to regard them as other than minor incidents within the existing order, was never more fatuously and self-sufficiently manifest.

Had the nation, a hundred and fifty years ago, shown any comprehensive prevision of the industrial revolution in which the old order was so soon to be overwhelmed, how much misery and how many problems of painful after-adjustment we might have been spared ! The new order was permitted to establish itself regardless of social ends and national purposes, unrecognized in its implications on national life until those implications had become explicit in established fact, and men held up their hands in horror at the industrial evils they had failed to foresee and might have avoided. The new machine industry became the master and the tyrant instead of the servant of human life, because its revolutionary powers were not recognized by the nation until they were in full and unchecked exercise. Are we, in face of unmistakable signs of revolutionary change, to repeat the experience of blind drift and haphazard, of refusing to believe that there can be any revolutionary change, until it comes upon us in a realization charged with evils and abuses from which national foresight might easily keep it clear ? Or is it to be intelligent guidance of the change, the benign advent of a new order in ways worthy of a nation claiming to be rational ? Of its coming in one way or the other—through confusion and disorder, if not by intelligent guidance—there is no longer the smallest possibility of doubt for clear-sighted men. The fools are a vast army, no doubt. But are we always, as a nation, to go the fools' way?

After which brief philosophic discursion on national frames of mind, let us proceed to a consideration of the Labour Unrest of these earlier years of the twentieth century, destined, I suggest to you, to take its place in history as the monumental example of obvious things unintelligible to contemporary understanding.

CHAPTER II

THE most cursory survey of industrial events during 1911 is enough to suggest to any thoughtful mind the existence of some general leaven at work in the world of Labour. An isolated strike, a dispute confined to a particular trade or a particular locality, might be set aside as of no more than sectional or local interest, a mere detail of no great importance in relation to the general movement of national life. But the Labour troubles of the present day are not capable of any such sectional or local explanation. The very phrase, " The Labour Unrest," reveals a consciousness of this fact in the general public mind, and its common use as the accepted descriptive term covering all these excursions and alarms is in itself a linking up of our present labour troubles into a single connected phenomenon, an implication of some common origin and provocation. There is no need to labour the point. Nobody with more than an idiot's power of counting beyond three and seeing the relationship between things, can believe our Labour troubles to be disconnected— mere casual incidents happening simultane- ously by some freak of chance.

And yet that is the crude view of the matter which many people, who would no doubt feel deeply insulted if you questioned their sanity, pretend to hold. The striker, in this view, is a turbulent and ignorant person, blind to his own best interests, who throws the affairs of a well-ordered community into confusion in mere recklessness and im- providence ; and what we call the Labour Unrest is simply the exhibition of his perver- sity. If you can shut your eyes to manifest facts sufficiently to persuade yourself into. that belief, it is, no doubt, a comforting illusion ; for it at once removes the whole business from the category of significant things, and makes it merely a question of police and of the firm handling of people whose intelligence is still in its infancy. A nuisance, no doubt ; but only of the sort that a nation may always expect to have to worry through in order to keep foolish persons within bounds.

How far this view of the matter is credulity and how far pretence it is not easy to say.

If one were to go by the newspapers—either
by the highly coloured reports in their news
columns or by the constant sermonizing of the
men in their editorial columns—one might
very well believe it to be a universally prevalent view.   But only a very small number of
very simple people take newspapers seriously
nowadays.   So far as general repute is concerned, the yellow press has ruined the credit
of English journalism beyond retrieving.
When first the era of the intoxicated headline
and the daily booming sensation dawned upon
us, the public, accustomed in some degree to
rely upon statements purporting to be statements of fact in newspapers, bore up for a
while under the daily strain upon its credulity.   But when it began to find out that
Pekin legations massacred in Fleet Street
in the most circumstantial detail one day,
were living and uninjured in next week's
editions, and that Monday's sensation was
generally dropped by Wednesday on evidence
of its falsity, and a new Wednesday sensation
concocted in order to divert attention from it,
the public began to suspect.   It is now,
fortunately, generally known that the modern
newspaper does not even pretend to purvey
news, but only to write up news from one
violently partisan point of view or another,

and in a form lending itself to sensational headlines and catch-halfpenny placards ; that if the actual news of the day does not lend itself to that treatment the business of an up-to-date sub-editor and reporter is to concoct news which will ; and that the whole thing is a distorting mirror deliberately curved and shaped so as to reflect the movement of the world's affairs as a face is reflected in a spoon. The newspaper of one party holds up the concave side of the spoon, and the newspaper of the other party the convex side, with the result that the same movement which appears in one as all brow and intellect, appears in the other as all nose and jaw. You pay your halfpenny and you take your choice.

With regard to Labour movements, however, the newspapers are largely controlled by financial interests on the anti-Labour side in this class war, and consequently reflect it adversely. There are exceptions, newspapers which still hold by an honourable tradition of truthfulness in the presentment of the news of the day ; but for the most part the distortion of news bearing upon Labour movements is pronounced in such a degree as to be positively grotesque. The reporter who goes out to record an incident in the labour unrest, the sub-editor who puts headlines to it and fits it into the news columns, the leader writer who comments upon it, all know perfectly well that they would lose their jobs if they represented the matter in any other aspect than the aspect required by the proprietary interests of the paper. Not only the class interests of newspaper proprietors, but the class feelings of the advertisers, have to be considered. The newspaper lives on its advertisers, and the paying advertiser is, in the vast majority of cases, a person financially interested as employer on the anti-Labour side of these disputes. The distortion of the mirror is inevitable under such conditions.

But while the newspaper view of the matter is quite obviously pretence rather than credulity, pretence kept up deliberately as a safeguard for the proprietary interests of the country against the dissemination of dangerous ideas, amongst the ruck of the propertied classes it is probably genuine credulity rather than pretence. The responsible men of the propertied classes, those who are actually engaged in the great game of exploiting industry, know perfectly well what this movement means. But the mob of propertied people are not responsibly engaged in enterprises. The development of the joint-stock company system has made the mass of property owning functionless in the modern world, so far as active personal participation in affairs is concerned. In the modern class of investors and shareholders we have succeeded in producing the most timorously stupid class in the history of any civilization, a class regarded as the legitimate prey of all the shark professions, a class for whom it is the daily business of commercial and financial enterprise to set successful booby-traps. And it is this class which supplies what is commonly described as the sound business judgment of the country. It has been assured of that so constantly by every shrewd rascal who sets out to make money out of its stupidity that it has come to believe it of itself, and to regard itself as the depository of whatever sanity and sobriety of judgment now exists in national affairs. Its standard of judgment is a very simple one. Its absorbing concern in life is to discover that sacred spot, on the margin between security and insecurity in its investments, where dividend is highest, and to pitch its tent there. It is sensitive to movements in industrial life, to human ideals and philosophies of social organization, solely and only by their effect upon that sacred margin.

If they push the frontier further out so as to include more dividend within the limits of security, they are divine movements, evidence of the care which Providence bestows upon the class which is the salt of the earth. If they move the frontier inwards, compelling the class which is the salt of the earth to move its tents back into a region of less dividend, on pain of being left in the frightful outside desert of insecurity, they are movements and philosophies born of the devil, and all the electoral power of the sound business judgment of the country must be concentrated against them. It is on this frontier that commercial and financial enterprise does its business with these sheep, spreading its lures and baits and setting its booby-traps in profusion ; and the investor and shareholder class spends its life in alternately nibbling forward at more dividend and still more dividend, and then rushing back in a panic when the springing of the traps reveals the fact that the sheep have been lured over the border, and that they are lucky who get back alive or unfleeced.

With such an outlook upon the world and upon human destiny, this class provides a public opinion and an electoral influence of enormous value to the more active predatory spirits of the day, an opinion and an influence flung for all it is worth against any movement of Labour Unrest which, by seeking for the wage-earner a larger proportion of the good things of life, threatens to restrict the exploitation of the worker. It is an opinion and an influence to which the idea of a human craving for fuller life amongst the disinherited class is quite incomprehensible. It sees such a craving only in terms of its possible effect upon dividends and the security of investments. Hence it can be used as a most powerful weapon by the shrewder exploiters, the masters of the game, who know what they are after and what the whole game of labour-exploitation amounts to ; and it is mainly to keep it in a state of efficient electoral terror against Labour that the newspaper reflection of events in the Labour world is kept up to the necessary degree of distortion, and that the credulity of the people of this class is constantly lubricated by glorification of their sound business judgment in these matters.

But even a credulity so impervious to facts as this is, begins to wear somewhat thin against current events ; thin enough, at any rate, to enable most people to distinguish, as all but the stone-blind can distinguish,

c

between light and the absence of light. Only eyes of horn can fail to discern, if not the actual significance, at least the presence of significance in these events. Take the record of 1911. We began the year with the miners' strike in South Wales. Following that came the international strike of seamen and the general upheaval amongst all sections of transit workers. Here, there, and everywhere dockers, carters, carmen, lightermen, tramway workers, porters in various trades, women workers, engineers, and a host of labourers attached to various industries were withholding their labour for better conditions, or bargaining for improvements under the imminent threat of striking. Rioting, in many cases accompanied by bloodshed, became a daily feature in the news reports. The disorders in Liverpool, which seemed to be the culminating point of the trouble, were immediately followed by the much more serious and widespread war in the railway world ; and for a couple of days in August the whole, or nearly the whole, of our internal communications were so obstructed as to throw the general business of the nation into confusion. At that date over 370,000 workmen were directly involved in the various disputes ; and a much larger number indirectly. So serious was the position that the Government, in a panic, placed the troops of the nation at the disposal of the employers, and practically superseded municipal responsibility for keeping the peace in a number of towns ; in many cases, as in Manchester, against the emphatic protests of the responsible local authorities. It was, for the moment, actual war. Although the strike was ended, and the railwaymen induced to return to work, it was not ended by a settlement of the dispute, but only by a promise of prompt reference of the dispute to a Royal Commission, sitting day in and day out to consider the matter. The issue of the report of the Commission was received with derision by the great majority of the men, and all the evidence shows that the unrest amongst them, so far from being settled, has been intensified by the exasperation at having been manœuvred, as the men believe, out of the victory which they are convinced was within their grasp in August. The year closes with this ominous feeling widespread throughout the railway service, with a lock-out of cotton operatives on a great scale in Lancashire, and with a ballot in progress amongst the miners which may involve a general strike in the coal-getting industry before the winter closes.

These are only the main outstanding incidents of our domestic record in this year of
industrial revolt.   Of the scores of minor
disputes accompanying these major hap-
penings it is not necessary to speak.
Hardly a district has been free from
them, and they have ranged over most
industries.

Serious as such a record is, we should miss
something of its gravity if we failed to note
that these events in our own country have
had their parallel, in more or less degree, in
other countries.   There have been labour
troubles everywhere ; strikes in France, bread
riots in Austria, vast demonstrations against
the increased cost of living and a tremendous
spread of Socialism in Germany, an astonishing series of Socialist successes in the United
States local elections, successes which have
transferred the local administration of district
after district to the new Labour and Socialist
forces which seem to be marching from
strength to strength in every civilized country.
Nor can the political upheavals of the world
be kept out of the record of the year of
insurrection.   Events in China, in Portugal,
in Turkey, in Mexico ; can any one doubt
that these also are manifestations in kind
of the new world-spirit of which the wide-

spread labour troubles of 1911 are the industrial expression ?

Taking the picture as a whole, is it conceivable that any theory of mere sporadic recklessness and improvidence can cover it ? The comfortable delusion that the Labour Unrest brings us face to face with a problem of no more serious import than the thoughtless ignorance of what is for their own good of a few men here and a few men there, led astray by well-fed agitators living comfortably on the credulity of their dupes, will not do. Indeed, it will not do.

Slightly more intelligent is the public opinion which admits the existence of certain grievances behind the unrest. But for the most part, this opinion regards strikes with the same sort of deprecation as they are regarded by the cruder opinion which puts the whole thing down to ignorant and agitator-fostered recklessness. The social reformer who seeks to deal with those grievances by steady and well-considered legislation is all right, but strikes are only a passing frenzy, in this view of the matter ; in which there is no more conception, generally speaking, of fundamental social and industrial changes in progress than there is in the cruder view. In both cases there is the underlying idea that our first business is to get industrial peace, a settlement of whatever the immediate dispute may be ; and that with that settlement the industrial world will go on its normal way as before ; with a little easement here, perhaps, and a little re-adjustment there, but on the same main lines of social organization.

That is the widely prevalent crude view of the Labour Unrest. And before we can discuss the whole matter intelligently, it is necessary to clear the ground of the illusions upon which that view is based.

First, as to the settlement of disputes. The illusion here is that any settlement of a labour dispute is a good thing so long as work is resumed. The one thing is to get the strike over, or to prevent the threat of a strike from culminating in an actual stoppage of work. Whether the men secure concessions or not, whether admitted grievances remain or go, whatever the terms of settlement may be, surrender or success or compromise, it is assumed that " industrial peace " is the same thing as the ending of the strike. On the announcement that such and such a strike is over and that work is resumed, we have the usual hymn of thanksgiving in all the newspapers over the settlement.

The assumption in all this apotheosis of the peacemaker and supposition that the ending of a strike is a good thing in itself on any terms, is that there has been no real contest of interests in the struggle, no problem other than that of freakishness on the part of those responsible for the stoppage of work. The strike is a nuisance ; get it over and done with.

It is not necessary to go beyond the record of the unrest in the railway world to see the short-sightedness and fallaciousness of this view. Settlements of disputes on that basis are no settlements at all.

It was the " settlement " of 1907 which kept the railway service in a condition of ferment and unrest leading up to the worse outbreak of 1911. And the " settlement " of 1911 carries with it the certainty of a still worse outbreak later on. It is one thing to end a strike, and quite another thing to secure conditions of stability in an industry ; and every strike which is settled without removing the irritation which produced it, so far from being a step towards industrial peace, is a preliminary to worse disorders.

The history of the railway unrest is worth recording in some detail for its bearing upon this point. It was in October of 1907 that the railwaymen decided to enforce, by strik-

ing, their demand for the recognition of their
union, as a means by which they could
negotiate more effectively with the railway
companies for increased wages and reductions
in the hours of labour.   The ballot of the men
gave 76,925 votes in favour of a strike and
8,778 against.   What happened on that occasion will be within the general public recollection.   The companies refused to meet the
union representatives, and the general railway
strike was on the point of taking place when
Mr. Lloyd George, then President of the
Board of Trade, intervened as peacemaker,
and, after consultation with the railway
directors, submitted to the men's representatives a conciliation scheme which did not
concede a single one of the men's demands.
The railway directors naturally backed the
scheme, for it was mainly their own proposal.
It not only refused the demand for recognition
of the union, but it broke up the possibility
of all-grades action by the men, by providing
that only proposals affecting each grade
separately should come before the Conciliation Boards for consideration ; and it further
tied the men down for seven years from the
possibility of striking.   The trade union
representatives, with the definite mandate of
their men to declare a strike if the negotia-

tions failed to secure recognition, lost their heads at the critical moment, and under the tremendous pressure of the Board of Trade and the railway directors acting together, consented to the Conciliation Scheme. The strike was avoided, and every newspaper in the kingdom broke out into pæans of praise of Mr. Lloyd George, the peacemaker, the conciliator, the genius who had given us seven years' assured peace in the railway world.

Within six months, while the echoes of the hymns of praise were still resounding, everybody knew that there had been no settlement, no conciliation, no lasting peace. So far from having stopped the unrest, the Conciliation Scheme intensified it. The men had got nothing, and went about their work with the exasperated feeling of having been plausibly tricked out of concessions which they believed they could have enforced but for the way in which their representatives had been out-manœuvred and outwitted in the negotiations over the Conciliation Scheme. The peace patched up in that way in 1907 led directly to the chaos of 1911. Instead of dealing with the whole question on its merits, the so-called settlement of 1907 simply pretended that the only issue was, not to settle grievances, but

to settle the strike.   The master stroke of
the 1907 settlement—the pledging of the men's
representatives to accept the Conciliation
Scheme for a period of seven years—was hailed
as a special triumph for industrial peace,
inasmuch as it gave, in addition to the immediate avoidance of the threatened strike, a
promise of enduring peace.   The event proved
it to be indeed a master-stroke, but a master-
stroke effective in exactly the opposite direction; for it has been the feeling of having
been manœuvred out of the right of fighting
that has been one of the chief exasperations
of the men, one of the most provocative of the
causes of the outbreak of 1911.   Instead of
dealing with the disorder, the settlement of
1907 suppressed for the moment the strike
symptom of the disorder, leaving the disorder
itself to work like poison within the system,
all the more virulently because of the stoppage
of its natural outlet.

And so it is with all these settlements which
leave grievances unremedied.   They are no
settlements.   The very first thing to be clearly
understood, if we are to have any intelligent
public understanding of the Labour Unrest,
is that the strikes are not the unrest, but only
the symptoms of the unrest ; that the ending
of a strike is not necessarily an advantage,

and may quite conceivably be a worsening of the disorder ; and that the primary question which has to be faced is that of the demands behind the strike—whether they are just and worth fighting for. Only in its bearing upon that aspect of the matter can we judge aright whether a settlement is a real settlement or only a banking-up of the fires of disorder for a fiercer outbreak a little later.

A second consideration to be carefully noted in passing, as a preliminary to the real discussion of the problem, is as to the character of strikes and of strikers. The illusion which prevails about this is due to the utter inability of the secure person to put himself in the place of the weekly wage-earner. No person living in security can have any really adequate idea of what striking means to the man who has to make the momentous decision whether he will " down tools " or not. But, while his understanding of the workman's position may fall very far short of adequacy, it ought, with ordinary common sense and even the least power of imagination, to be sufficient to guard him against the foolish notion that strikes on any large scale can be light-heartedly undertaken in a spirit of mere recklessness. For who are the strikers ? They are not only the casually employed persons, men accustomed to be in work to-day and out of a job to-morrow, who have become dehumanized and callous to the precariousness of casual employment, as eels are said to become accustomed to skinning. Men like railwaymen, engineers, carters, and many others who have been involved in recent strikes, are, for the most part, men in settled employment, men with homes and wives and children absolutely dependent upon their retention of their employment and the weekly wage they get for it ; men with rooted associations, domestic and social, in their town or district. Many of them have been all their working days in the same employment. The whole settled structure of their lives is dependent on their fixity of service. When such men strike, they stake their lives upon the hazard. They risk everything. Let the secure person imagine, if he can, even though it be but dimly, the conditions under which such men approach the decision to strike. Take the ballot of the railway workers, which I have already quoted, as an example, in which 76,925 men voted for the strike and 8,778 against. The railway directors, I know, point out that a large proportion of railwaymen are not in the unions, and are therefore outside this vote altogether. But the men who are outside the unions are, for the most part, the more casual men and the lower grades—porters in the country districts and the like. The men who are most solidly in the unions are the skilled permanent men—the engine-drivers, signalmen, firemen, guards, and the like. These are the men who voted in the proportion of nine to one for striking ; men with a settlement, with homes and permanent associations. Every social and domestic tie was against the likelihood of their giving such a vote lightly. Whether they would ever get back again into settled employment if once they came out was uncertain. It is conceivable that here and there an exceptionally irresponsible man might vote for striking in a spirit of recklessness ; but it is not conceivable that a whole class of men, a class amongst the most responsible of all our industrial classes, should do so ; and the person who believes it to be possible is incapable of forming a judgment on human motives and human conduct. Nothing but an overpowering sense of suffering from wrongs so great that it is worth while taking one's life in one's hand in order to get them righted, wrongs so deeply felt as to outweigh the security of settled livelihood, can account for such a vote, a vote which is only one example from many in the skilled industries.

And if it is sheer illusion to attribute these strike decisions to recklessness and indifference, it is equally illusion to ascribe them to the influence of the agitators. It is always the paid agitator, according to the capitalist press —the pestilent rascal who finds agitation an easier way of getting a comfortable living than working—who is at the back of these disputes, fattening on the pence of the deluded wage-earner. That ridiculous myth has been pretty completely exploded by the events of the past year or two. In any case, it is obvious that an agitator cannot create grievances, but can only voice them when they are actually there. He might agitate to all eternity without having the slightest effect upon the minds of men who have no grievance.

But one of the most significant facts about the unrest of the past year or two has been the repudiation of the agitators by the rank and file of the men. These ballots in favour of striking have, in industry after industry, been against the advice and influence of the agitators. The paid union official—to whose desire to justify his job strikes have been so generally attributed—has, for the most part, been a pacificator rather than an agitator.

It was the rank and file of the railwaymen who voted for striking in 1907, and the paid agitators who accepted the Conciliation Scheme against the strike mandate of the men. It was the paid agitator who discouraged and opposed the miners' strike in South Wales, and the rank and file of the men who turned the agitators out of office at the next election of union officers, not for agitating too much, but for agitating too moderately. It was the paid agitator, both trade union official and Parliamentary Labour representative, who not only consented to but actively worked for the stoppage of the railway strike last August, and the appointment of the farcical Royal Commission, which the men generally regarded as surrender and defeat ; and it was the paid agitator who, in the closing days of the year, accepted the report of the Royal Commission at the very moment when the ballot of the men was in progress, and suppressed the actual figures of the majority on that ballot against accepting it. Time and again, during the past two years, the strikes have broken out " without sanction," as it is called ; that is, without the approval of the agitators. If there is one thing more abundantly clear than another in all this, it is that working-class opinion does not recognize

the leadership of its agitators, but insists
upon regarding them, and upon their regarding themselves, as representatives and mouth-
pieces of the opinions and mandates conveyed
to them from the rank and file, as executive
officers acting under, instead of giving, guidance.   The Labour war has had its origin,
in the plainest possible way, not in agitation,
but in the decision and the common will of
the rank and file.

And those who know the trade union and
Labour movement best know how natural it is
that matters should work out in that way.
The mythical picture of the agitator, as it
exists in the imagination of the propertied
classes, is about as far from the facts as it
could possibly be.   The agitator's interest
is not to stir up industrial strife, but to keep
his office going as comfortably as possible
with a minimum of worry. His position
in the whole business, whether in his trade
union office or in Parliament—is not the
moderation and most gentleman-like be-
haviour · of the Labour M.P. universally
admired and held up as a model to all be-
holders ?—has been that of a conservative
and a restraining force, even to the point of
acting, over and over again, against the expressed mandate of those who pay him.

The outbreak has been from below, from
rank and file, the expression of a general
asperation, a movement of the people, born
their own impulses, their own reaching out,
wever blindly, however crudely, towards
her standards of life than they feel to be
ssible under existing industrial conditions.

Bearing in mind these few primary and
eliminary facts as to the characteristics of
Labour Unrest, characteristics which lie
the surface and are obvious, we can go on
consider the whole matter somewhat more
elligently than if we continued to talk in
lusive and complaisant myths about it.

CHAPTER III

IF we are to begin at the beginning in this investigation, it is necessary to go back a long way The preliminary observations made in the preceding chapter have had for their main purpose to bring home to the mind of the reader that the Labour Unrest is not merely a series of casual disputes, an isolated phenomenon of the past year or two, the fortuitous outcome of chance vexations in industry.   It is the latest phase of a connected and continuous movement going back over a century ; the movement which began with the coming of the machine industry, of which the industrial revolution that transformed England from a community of agriculturists and small handicraftsmen, working individually, to the England of huge manufacturing towns, the workshop of the world, was only the opening phase. From the beginning of the machine industry to the Labour Unrest of 1911 the process has been an orderly unfolding

34

of linked events in due sequence, an organic movement of growth towards a new social and industrial organization of the national life. And to see the Labour Unrest apart from the steadily developing movement of which it is an organic part is to see it falsely ; hardly even, indeed, to see it at all.

Already the movement, of which the Labour Unrest is the latest phase, has progressed so far that there is a temptation to fall into the illusory mood of historical retrospect about it, and to wonder why so obvious a development was not plainly seen from the very outset, and intelligently guided so as to avoid the complications and the unnecessary suffering through which the nation has had to pass in its advance to the end now so obvious for all who have eyes to see. Just as the transformation of England, accomplished between 1750 and 1850, from the handicraft to the manufacturing form of social organization, with all its ruthless effacement of institutions and habits of life regarded as immemorial within the old order, was visible in germ in the coming of the first machine, had there been the sufficient foresight amongst men to discern it ; so also does the completion of the process, the transformation from private capitalism to national control of industry, lie visibly in germ in the existing order ; a development dependent upon no new factors, but only upon the growth and expansion to their natural maturity of forces already operative within the existing order.

Events and incidents on the line of a great historic movement have their two causes. There is the general flow of the stream along which the whole thing moves, and there is the immediate provoking cause of this or that particular incident in the movement. Our shortsightedness, our constant surprise at developments which, in historic retrospect, are seen to have been clearly indicated from the very outset, is due to the fact that we are, for the most part, completely taken up with the immediate provoking causes of particular incidents, ignoring the general flow of the current. The immediate provoking causes may be, and very often are, casual and fortuitous ; but the moment they loosen men from their moorings of use and wont and inertia, the resultant action moves with and is governed by the general current. To those who desire to understand the movements of the day, the important thing is not to know the casual incident merely as a casual incident, but to see clearly what are the general, dominant, prevailing forces at work in men's minds and in society, shaping the ends to which all casual incidents contribute once they are loosened into action.

So it is with the Labour Unrest. For the most part, everybody is engaged in discussing, in trying to discover and to settle, the immediate provoking cause of this particular strike or that particular dispute. But the really important question is why such immediate provoking causes, often trivial and apparently haphazard, should lead to action in such a form and in such a direction. The immediate provoking causes no more explain the form and the direction of contemporary labour movements than the act of unmooring a boat explains why and at what rate it moves off in this or that direction. If you unmoor it at the edge of a stagnant pond, it will not move at all. It is the flow and force and direction of the current that can alone explain the movement. And it is the flow and force and direction of the current running in our industrial life which is the governing factor in connection with the Labour Unrest. What are the forces at work determining that direction ? What is the general and fundamental cause, obviously common to the age in every country where the wage system and the machine industry exist, underlying and giving the unity of a co-ordinated movement to the special and accidental minor circumstances of this dispute or that locality ?

Upon a clear understanding and an intelligent handling of these primary and determining forces depends whether or not the twentieth century will go down into history as an era of sane, prudent, rational development, or a period of blind and disorderly stumbling through difficulties. Of the final outcome there is no longer any possibility of doubt. But whether the new social order is to come by peaceful and reasonable progress or by a series of bitter contests and furious upheavals, depends entirely upon the degree of intelligence now shown by the nation in reading the indications aright and understanding the part which this generation is called upon to play in the great drama of human growth.

Let us, therefore, begin at the beginning, and endeavour to get a really comprehensive view of the Labour Unrest in its origins and in its historic setting. For you cannot get a true view of human affairs by instantaneous photograph. Even if you see the thing quite precisely as it is at the moment, it is still a false view, because the facts of movement and of growth do not come into the picture. For full understanding, it is necessary to know not only the immediate facts, but how they have come about, and by what long road men have come to such a frame of mind and to such actions as are expressed in the immediate facts.

A hundred years ago the new form of industrial civilization, born of the invention of machinery, had pretty well wiped the old feudal synthesis out of existence. For feudalism, with all its faults, was at any rate a synthesis, a social order. It recognized society as an organic whole, bound together by human duties and responsibilities. In the feudal conception of things, the lordship of a class was not an irresponsible thing detached from social duties ; it was part of the scheme for getting those social duties performed. Two forces brought about the decay of feudalism—the two forces always discernible in history when an old settled order goes down to ruin—weakness in character within and attack from without. An old order of society will go on existing in a rotten condition for generations, if free from attack. And new movements may go on attacking ineffectively from without if the old order remains sound in character and in its ability to serve the needs of human life. But when the attack from without is assisted

by the decay within, the old order falls.   So
it was with feudalism.   Founded from the
beginning upon a misinterpretation of human
nature, it had lost more and more its quality
of a social synthesis and had become a mere
class dominance ;   and when the attack came
upon it, by the growth of a new power of
wealth, non-territorial in form, the outcome
of the invention of machinery and the discovery of new forces applied to manufacture,
the end was inevitable.

The misinterpretation of human nature
upon which feudalism was founded was this.
Its ideal of society was the patriarchal ideal,
the ideal of the benevolent despot.   Given a
ruling class, that class was to be responsible
for the order of life ;   redressing wrongs, seeing
the King's justice was done, guaranteeing to
the people under it safety and protection in
return for service rendered by them.   The
virtues which its literature extolled were the
virtues of gentleness and courtesy, of un-
sullied honour, of bravery, of the sacredness of
its knightly word ;   a literature holding up the
ideal of conduct and of life according to the
feudal conception of a synthetic order of
things.   It pictured to itself the existence of
its ruling class as a shield held over the life
of the people, who were themselves pictured

as incapable of carrying on an ordered society to their own best advantage. The business of the good knight was to do his duty to the life of his estate quite as much as to receive duty and service from it. The one was the complement—nay, the essential condition—of the other.

Something of this old feudal conception of things still lingers in some rural districts left untouched by the modern manufacturing spirit ; and at its best it produced a human relationship compared with which the devil's chaos of life in a modern city of slums and factories is utterly contemptible.

The fatal weakness which doomed it from the outset, and which had become prevalent rottenness through and through by the time the attack came upon it from modern capitalism, was its assumption that any class of men are sufficiently removed from the frailties of selfish human nature to be entrusted with unchecked dominance over the life of a whole people. The feudal lord was ready enough to accept the privileges attaching to his lordship, and equally ready to neglect the responsibilities. Here and there, even down to the present day, an exceptional man, realizing that his position was essentially the position of a trustee, spent himself in service

to the life of his estate ; but for the most part
feudal lordship became a mere insistence upon
the rights and privileges of the lord, estates
became possessions for enjoyment and indul-
gence instead of trusts for the proper human
ordering and happiness of the life upon them ;
and the ideal of mutual service was lost in a
general oppression of the poor.

No stable social order will ever be built, as
feudalism attempted to build it, upon class
privilege. You may attach all the social
duties and responsibilities you please to the
possession of such class privilege ; but it is
in human nature that in the end the privilege
will be retained and the duty forgotten. So
it was with feudalism.

But all this might still have gone on, kept
in existence by the inertia of an existing order,
had it not been for the attack upon feudalism
from without. The feudal ruling class was a
territorial class. With the growth of trade
and manufacture a new form of wealth came
into existence, bringing with it a shifting of
population into great towns and an accumu-
lation of riches in the hands of a new class ;
and with riches, power. The centre of power
and of influence over the life of the country was
shifted. It became no longer dependent upon
territorial influences. With startling rapidity

it overthrew the old order ; and before society quite realized what was happening, a new force was dominant over the life of the nation.

And an appalling dominance it was. It acknowledged no social responsibility. Its one aim was to pile up wealth in the hands of individuals lucky enough or forceful enough to climb over their neighbours' heads into affluence. It claimed openly and deliberately that its operations should be outside the control of the State. It asserted its right to buy in the cheapest market and to sell in the dearest, asserted it as a new gospel of economic freedom. Its idea of buying in the cheapest market was to set children of five or six years old to work for next to nothing in its mines and factories. Any suggestion of regard for human life, of State intervention with a view to bringing these matters within such limits as would be tolerable to the national conscience, it resented as an interference with its devil's law of supply and demand. It claimed to set up its own new code of morality, and invented a pseudo-science of political economy —a description of the processes by which people unhampered by a conscience can get rich in a hurry—in which to expound the code. All it asked was to be let alone. If child labour was cheap, that was because child labour was plentiful, and the law of supply and demand must not be obstructed in its operations. If factories were dangerous and insanitary, that was because men, being free agents and no longer subject to the disgusting servility of feudalism, were willing to sell their labour under such conditions, and nobody had any right to interfere with their industrial freedom so to sell it. Thank God they were no longer living under the restrictions of a patriarchal system which prescribed conditions for them. They were emancipated into the joy of liberty. Leave things alone, and let the devil take the hindmost. Free competition, no State restrictions, supply and demand—these were the watchwords of the new order.

For a time this infernal gospel was supreme. And then, slowly but irresistibly, the stunned nation began to gather itself together into resistance to these ethics of hell, and to set to work to bring the new forces of wealth production into a new social synthesis. The passing of the first Factory Act began the development of that new synthesis. For as soon as men woke up to the amazing thing which had so transformed their lives, their industry, their habits and institutions, they perceived that the new capitalism was not a social synthesis at all. It was not a new social order, but the denial of the right of a social order to exist at all ; the dissolving of national organization, the establishment of chaos under the name of free competition. It had insisted that the resources of the nation, instead of being available for the national life, should be turned into stakes for individual gamblers, regardless of the collective life of society. When the nation, happily having something of a conscience left, began to look into the conditions of life in its industrial districts, it began immediately to deny the validity of the new gospel of individual grab as the divinely appointed method of conducting the affairs of a civilized and sane community ; and the long fight began against the devilish theory that the production of wealth should be independent of any consideration of the justice of the conditions under which it is produced or of its effect upon human life. The first Factory Act was the first effort towards a new social order ; feeble, trivial, and, as we shall see as the enquiry proceeds, missing the effective road, but still a beginning, an effort towards bringing the organisation of the new material resources of the nation into conformity with the requirements of human life and the demands of social justice.

Had the men of that time but hit upon the right road, we should have been spared a century of effort largely wasted and experiments mostly futile ; and we should not to-day be face to face with the problem of the Labour Unrest. With the apparently incurable instinct of human nature for avoiding root causes, and dealing with the surface symptoms of an evil, they adopted a method which led us for a century wandering in by-paths which have always brought us tortuously round to the same problem again. It was probably necessary to exhaust the possibilities of error in this way, necessary in the conditions under which the human mind works, and helpful in the end in giving the guarantee of an assured certainty to the final phases of the solution of the problem ; the final phases through which we are now rapidly passing.

But while the error of method which began with the first Factory Act is now patent to all observers ; while it is clear that everything done in that direction has still left us face to face with the fundamental evils against which men's consciences revolted, modified a little here and there in detail, but unchanged in their essential features—the division of society

into rich and poor, the failure to make the
constantly expanding resources of the nation
available for the general life of the nation, the
hunger of children, the unemployment and
destitution of men, the recruiting of resourceless women into prostitution, the horrible
slum life of every industrial town—while it
is clear that the fundamental facts, though
slightly regulated and trimmed of some of their
filthiest cruelties, remain untouched in their
essentials, nevertheless the important thing
to note at the moment is the fact of the moral
revolt against the new capitalism and its
gospel of free competition.

That revolt has never ceased since then.
It is the clue to the whole political, social,
and industrial history of the nineteenth century. It is the motive which gives unity and
coherence to all the struggles for enfranchisement, for political rights, for education, for
trade unionism, and for the betterment of
industrial conditions, which have made the
nineteenth century the era of awakening
democracy ; and it alone explains the Labour
Unrest of our day, enabling us to see that unrest in its historic origins and connections, in
its co-ordination with what has gone before
and its significance for the future.

CHAPTER IV

ITS ETHICAL BASIS

IT is necessary at this point in the argument to sum up, briefly but emphatically, the moral characteristics of this movement of revolt which has been the life of the nineteenth century, the vital motive of national action. We have seen how and under what circumstances it arose ; how the ending of an old order of things which, at least in its conception of national life, was a true synthetic order, was followed by a moral disintegration and a period of no order at all ; how the new forces of wealth production and of the power of riches, new permanent forces to which human life must ultimately adjust itself, and consistently with which human happiness must be attained if it is to be attained at all, how these new forces came in an irruption without any adjustment to human needs ; how the old social organisation gave place to a chaotic individual scramble for wealth regardless of social consequences, and how the very idea of any social organization at all, beyond an organization of police to keep the ring for the scramblers, was challenged in the name of free competition, the right of the hindmost to go to the devil and of the most efficiently predatory to thrust him there.

The simple elementary fact that this is not the devil's world, but ultimately and triumphantly God's world, and that whoever falls for a moment under the delusion that it is otherwise is a fool and a simpleton, is the primary underlying fact to be borne in mind in interpreting human history. And since it is to men, in the working out of their human instincts, that the insistence upon God's purpose of order and of justice in the world is committed, the human revolt against the new fools' gospel of getting rich by buying in the cheapest market and selling in the dearest followed naturally and inevitably upon the temporarily successful raid of the powers of darkness by which Mammon-worship superseded Christianity as the established religion of the new capitalist world. Mrs. Browning's " Cry of the Children " will remain for all time the human record of that brief empire of the devil on earth, the blasting exposure of the life in hell, as against the life

E

God fashions and reveals, that men have to
live when they forget.

The revolt was not merely against this or
that incident of cruelty or child murder or
injustice perpetrated in the name of the new
gospel. It was a revolt against the new
gospel itself in its essential teaching, against
the whole outlook on human life and human
destiny for which the new gospel stood.
Study its expression in the literature of the
first half of the nineteenth century, a literature in which all that was best and noblest in
English life was rallied to the crusade against
the defacement of God's temple in human
form perpetrated day by day in the wild-beast
scramble for wealth, and the essential character of the revolt will become clear enough
to you. The moral inspiration of the revolt
was in its perception of the fact that, if the
world be truly God's world and by no means
the devil's empire, the real purpose of industry
cannot be the making of individual men rich
regardless of social consequences, but the
development of the resources of the country
for the promotion of the happy and rational
life of its people.

There, then, are the two opposing philosophies, the two outlooks on human life, between
which the battle of the nineteenth century has

been fought out ; at bottom a moral and religious struggle, without a clear understanding of which the political and industrial history of the nineteenth century is an unintelligible maze of casual and purposeless incidents.

At the outset it looked as though the new dominant and triumphant capitalism was to have it all its own way, that the moral order of life in England was permanently destroyed, and the new industrial hell was established for ever as our irrevocable way of life. That, of course—always remembering that it is God's world—was an impossible thing, the dream of an imbecile. But how securely it seemed to have established itself, and how helpless human life appeared to be against it for the moment !

It is impossible to exaggerate the debt which the world owes to John Ruskin for his work at that moment of apparent hopeless defeat for the claims of human life against the claims of cash. When he began to voice those principles of human life in relation to wealth-getting which have so largely helped to create the effective revolutionary sentiments of to-day, he was received with contempt and derision. " The appearance of a man of genius may be gathered from the virulence of dunces," says

Macaulay ; and the dunces—dunces none the less because they were crowned and supreme for the moment—surely never had such a vituperative innings as when Ruskin began to publish his challenge to the orthodox political economy of his day. So great was the clamour that two of the leading reviews, having begun to publish instalments of his work, refused to go on with him, in deference to the abuse which was showered upon them for printing such pestilent nonsense as Ruskin's views were deemed to be. He was hopelessly wrong, entirely contrary to received opinion, condemned by all reasonable folk, a man gone crazy. " Political economy is one thing and ethics is another ; and nothing is to be gained by confusing them," wrote one recognized authority on political economy, with an air of finally disposing of Ruskin's absurdities.

That was the very blasphemy against which Ruskin raised his holy war. It was the accepted gospel of the day. It handed over the whole of our industrial affairs to a soulless competition, with the one injunction upon it to get rich, to get rich in a hurry, to get rich without regard for the ethical validity of its operations. Its test and standard of commercial activity was not whether it was just, but whether it would pay. It set up the silly notion, dear to the minds of all dunces, that a nation is rich if only it has so many millions' worth of material property.

What Ruskin told it, with damnable reiteration, was that its riches were only real wealth according to the way in which they were acquired and the purposes to which they were applied. The test of wealth must be an ethical test. Unjustly acquired or wrongly applied, riches, so far from being the wealth, are the poverty of a nation, the bankruptcy and destitution of a nation. Such riches are the elements of death rather than of life, shackles and fetters of a prison house rather than the equipment of men for free human existence. You cannot say whether a nation is well or badly off merely by knowing that it has so many million pounds' worth of property, unless you know what that property is ethically. It may be so many million tons' weight of tombstone built over the grave of the nation. If it is in the form of forty million pounds' worth (market value) of slum dwellings, the community is poorer by its existence, filthier, less human, less wealthy; and would be wealthier, in the only real wealth of human life, by its disappearance. To the orthodox political economist, the market

value in hard cash is the only test of wealth.
To Ruskin, the ennoblement of human life
was the only real test. " There is no wealth
but life ; life, including all its powers of
love, of joy, of admiration. That country is
the richest which nourishes the greatest
number of noble and happy human beings."

In that great saying Ruskin summed up the
conflict of the age. Understood in all its
implications, it illumines and explains the
whole story of the nineteenth century, and
makes plain the nature of the struggle now
rounding to its completion. It defines the
purpose of organized human life and of
wealth production in terms of absolute and
irreconcilable opposition to the terms imposed upon the nation by the new capitalism ;
and our age only becomes intelligible when
we see its incidents in relation to the endeavour
to bring our institutions, our political and
industrial organization, into conformity with
that purpose.

It is a challenge to the economics of the
modern gospel of wealth-getting, not upon
any minor issue of detail, but on the capital
issue. The fight between these two opposing
theories of human conduct in industrial
affairs is a fight to the death ; essentially an
ethical fight, as all the great struggles are in

human history, for the possession of the soul of the people.

I can imagine readers of this book, taking it up in the expectation of finding it devoted exclusively to the discussion and examination of the material facts of the Labour Unrest, wondering what in the world a discussion on primary ethics and religion has to do with the subject. We shall have our discussion on the material facts of the problem before we are through with it ; but, meanwhile, it is necessary to assure, with all gentleness, those who think to approach the matter understandingly without taking into account the primary ethical and religious origin and character of the whole movement, that they are not of the lineage to whom it is given to approach any problem of human conduct understandingly. For it is by this approach to the question, and by this alone, that understanding is to be achieved, and the material facts seen clearly for what they are.

CHAPTER V

THE STATUS OF THE WORKER

BEGINNING with a clear understanding of the direct conflict in morals underlying this great struggle, and of the essentially ethical character of the whole movement, we are now in a position to go on to the direct investigation of the economic and material facts. And here again the historical method of investigation is imperative. It is perfectly useless to imagine that by looking at the contemporary facts in isolation from all that has gone before we can arrive at any valid knowledge of them. We must trace the thing up from its origins and through its processes of development if we are to know anything worth knowing about it as it faces us at the moment.

Let us begin, therefore, by endeavouring to get as clear a picture as possible into our minds of the economic position of the wage-earner at the period, say, from a hundred to a hundred and twenty years ago, when the new industrialism, based on the new machine methods of production, may be regarded as having definitely established itself.

Let us at the moment attempt to draw no moral from it, but simply to ascertain the plain facts as to the nature of the industrial organisation in which the mass of the people found themselves set down to live their lives in the world. Let us leave out of account the excessive cruelties of the time, the story of child labour, of unfenced machines and the danger to life which prevailed in every factory, and all that aspect of the matter which may be regarded as the intemperance of the new industrial system in its pursuit of profits. What we want to get at are its essential characteristics, a clear definition of the economic relationship of the wage-earner to society at that moment.

Penetrating as deeply as we can to the foundations, the primary fact to be noted is that of the nature of the new tools. They were tools which could not be individually handled by individual men, tools which required aggregations of men for their operation, massed labour instead of separate independent workers.

That is the primary fact to be noted, and from it follows the consequential fact as to ownership of the new tools. The separate independent worker, carrying on an individual handicraft, could own and control his own individual tools. In the new machine industry he could not.

Putting these two constituent facts together, the curtain of the new industrial drama rises at the opening of the nineteenth century upon a working population separated from ownership of the means of its work. The two necessary factors in production, capital and labour, stand apart.

And the second thing to be noted is the enormously increased power of wealth production made possible by the new tools. Adding to the actual labour engaged the cost of the new tools and the cost of the new supervising, organising, and co-ordinating processes required by the substitution of massed labour for separate individual work, the resultant wealth production had become enormously greater in proportion to the expenditure of time and of labour ; including everything in labour, from invention and supervision down to the last manual operation in the whole process.

Here, then, so far as wealth production is concerned, we see this community of workers of all grades raised to a new level of power.

In the same time and with the same expenditure of energy, they were producing wealth many times over greater in quantity than they could have done before the coming of the machine.

And yet we see them in deep poverty, living from hand to mouth at the lowest margin of subsistence and under the most squalid conditions of herding in uncared-for urban quarters rapidly spreading like disease blotches over the face of the country. The first Factory Act was passed in 1802, and the immediate cause of its passing was the fearful spread, throughout the factory district of Manchester, of epidemic disease, which made terrible havoc amongst the working population, and especially amongst the working child population, " on account of their scanty mode of living and way of working," says the historian of the period. The factory areas, we read, were " notorious for their unhealthiness and filthy condition," and the first report issued by a Board of Health appointed in the Manchester district under these conditions, pointed to the crowding of workmen in factories as the direct and chief source of the epidemic fevers which prevailed.

I do not quote these facts by way of calling attention to the excesses of capitalism, but

only to emphasise the primary fact that
while the wealth-producing powers of any
given number of workers had enormously
increased, we find them living in a condition
of poverty and squalor clearly indicative of
the fact that the increased wealth production
was not getting into the lives of the pro-
ducers. The higher power of production
was not accompanied by a higher power of
living ; that remained at bare subsistence,
with a new detestable quality of urban squalor
and filth added.

And so our attention must necessarily
pass from the facts of wealth production to
the facts of wealth distribution, if we are
clearly to see what was the economic relation
of the worker to society at that stage in the
development of the industrial revolution.

The governing factor in distribution was
that which we have already noted—the fact
of the separation of labour from ownership
over its own tools and materials. Let us
examine closely and particularly the effect
of that separation upon the process of wealth
distribution.

Not being the owner of his own tools and
materials, it followed that the worker was
also not the owner of his product.   He had no
direct interest whatever in his own product.

It belonged exclusively to the owner of the tools and materials, and passed automatically out of the hands of the worker as fast as he embodied his labour in it. Three factors went to the making of the completed product. First, the new tools, the factor contributed by the age, by the growth of knowledge and invention. Although we speak of this man's invention and that man's discovery, no single man invented more than a finishing touch here and a little detail there added to what had gone before. The new tools were the product of the generally growing knowledge of the age, the work of myriads of men, each adding a little to the constantly accumulating store of invention, each building upon the labour of others and upon the common stock of the day's expanding knowledge. Secondly, the factor of organization, of getting together tools and materials and labour in the enterprise of production. And thirdly, the labour of the worker engaged in the process, as distinguished from the speculative enterprise, of production. Of these three factors, two are seen at once to be essential in the form in which they were actually used ; the labour of the worker, without which there could be no production at all, and the new tools, the contribution of the community as a whole,

of the inventive spirit of the age and the
common stock of knowledge, to the process
of production ; without which factor production would have remained at its lower handicraft level without increase.   But the remaining factor, though essential in itself as a factor
of organization, is equally clearly seen not to
have been an essential factor in the actual
form which it took, the form of exclusive
ownership separated from labour and from
invention.   A co-operating community could
have contributed that factor equally well,
so far as the essential of organization is
concerned, and in that form prevented the
disastrous separation between the interests
of capital and labour by combining them in
the same body of people, the disastrous
separation from which the whole of the trouble
has arisen.

Thus, following the process of distribution,
we find this remarkable condition of affairs ;
that of the three contributory parties to
production, the foremost, the general community, from whose common stock of knowledge and spirit of invention the whole of the
increase in productive power came, had no
interest in the product at all and no concern
with the business, while the worker, a portion
of whose life, an actual part of himself, went in

labour power into the completed product, received only a bare subsistence without any relation to the value of the product, which passed exclusively into the possession of the third party, whose contribution was only the accidental form rather than the essential factor of organization.

This process of distribution was completely governed and brought about by the ownership of the tools being separate from the labour operating them. The worker, in that process of distribution, ceased to be a human factor at all, and became a commodity in the market. He was merely so much purchasable labour power, in the same category as tools and materials ; not one of the human sharers in industry, but one of the expenses of production to be met by the owner.

And his price in the labour market was settled in the ordinary way by supply and demand. The supply of resourceless persons being large, and they being under the immediate compulsion of hunger to sell their labour without being able to hold out for a favourable market, the price was low ; just as low as subsistence permitted, and regulated by the cost of maintenance.

The economic relationship of the worker to society was, therefore, not a human relation-

ship at all ; but the relationship of a saleable
commodity, of a very perishable sort, to an
over-supplied market. His footing in industry
was not that of a citizen interested in the
resources of the nation and in their increase
and application to human life, but simply
that of being permitted a bare maintenance
on condition of being lucky enough to catch
the eye of a labour-purchaser in the labour
market. He had that footing by no right of
his own as a man or a citizen, but only by
permission of an owner ; and on being admitted, he was required to produce his own
maintenance and a surplus in addition for the
owner ; the whole purpose and object of this
very remarkable form of industrial organization being to secure that surplus of profits
for the owner and to make it as great as
possible.

In a word, his position was that of a disinherited person. All the steadily increasing
power of wealth production passed him by.
He remained at the margin of subsistence,
and regarded himself as fortunate to secure
that rather than to be workless.

He was in the nation, but not of it. The new
activities of society were organized without
regard for him as a partner at all. He stood
in precisely the same economic relationship

to it as did the horse which drew his master's lorries. Like the horse, he had to be maintained, since without that his labour power would have ceased to be available. Had he been as physically strong, as effective for haulage, and as cheap in proportion to the amount of work he could do, he would undoubtedly have been set to the horse's work. He was no more a man in the transaction than the horse was a horse; they were both so much labour power, so much energy capable of being translated into work, labour power to be bought as a commodity as cheaply as possible, and to be set down in the accounts as one of the expenses of the business.

It is necessary to fasten with the clearest possible understanding upon this fundamental economic relationship of the worker to society at the outset of the new industrial system. It is the key to the whole economic problem. To grasp its essential character as a relationship between men in organized society, to comprehend it in all its implications, to see how it follows inevitably from the private ownership of the new tools, is a necessary preliminary to any understanding of nineteenth century history and of the position in which we now stand.

That, then, was the economic position of the non-owning working class ; a position of disinheritance.   And the problem created by the industrial revolution, the problem set for civilization to solve, the problem over which the struggle has been raging ever since, is the problem of so adjusting the economic relationship of the worker to society as to make all the human interests concerned in wealth production sharers and inheritors of the new wealth ; to make that new wealth the servant of human life instead of its master and tyrant.

It is already evident at this stage in the enquiry that the evil is not in the excesses and intemperances of capitalism, but in the fundamentally wrong and dehumanized position in which it places labour in organized society.   The evil is the primary evil of the status of the worker, and the detailed injustices which have excited the horror of all good men and women are only the symptoms and disclosures of that primary evil.

The fallacy which invalidates the whole of the political economy of that period—the extraordinary literature in which the apologists of the new order attempted to exalt into irrevocable laws of nature the methods of wealth production and distribution which were inflicting so much misery on the mass of the people—was the fallacy of taking this primary evil for granted, and only arguing within it as to what were and what were not possible and profitable methods of wealth production. Beginning with the assumption, unquestioned and even unnoted, so blindly was it taken for granted, that private ownership of the means of the nation's work was the natural order of things, and that human labour was simply a commodity, the economists of the period had no difficulty in showing that labour, like every other commodity, must be content to have its price fixed by supply and demand ; that since labour was plentiful and must seek a purchaser at once because of its perishable dependence upon daily food, it must recognise the iron law of wages which kept its price at the margin of subsistence ; and that to imagine it could be otherwise was to fly in the face of the natural laws of wealth production.

The fact is, of course, as a moment's reflection will show you, that there are no such laws of wealth production and wealth distribution binding upon a human society as can be compared with natural laws ; and the attempt of political economy to claim that sort of authority for its descriptions of the processes by which men can become rich under capitalism

is pure nonsense. There is no such thing as
an absolute law of political economy with
regard to the distribution of wealth. The
distribution of wealth depends entirely upon
human desire and purpose in the organization
of society ; and every such desire and purpose
has its own distinct political economy.   Thus,
you can have the economics of competition or
the economics of co-operation, the economics
of private ownership or the economics of
national ownership.   Given a certain form of
social and industrial organization, the business
of political economy is to discover what are the
most efficient methods of carrying on that
form of organization, what are the processes
by which competition or co-operation work
most effectively.   But whether the competi-
tive or the co-operative form of organized
society is best for human life is a question to
be settled by ethical considerations, by human
desire as to the kind of life men set up as
their ideal.   The orthodox political economy
begins by assuming that question to have
been settled in favour of private capitalism,
and so goes on to propound its laws of private
capitalist wealth production and distribution
as if they were laws of the universe, and to
talk about supply and demand as applied to
the price of labour as if it were comparable

with the law of gravitation. No doubt it is, if you begin by assuming for labour the status of a commodity in a universe of privately owned capital. In precisely the same way, as Ruskin has pointed out, if you begin by assuming that men have no skeletons, you could write the most interesting treatises on how to roll them into pellets or stretch them into cables. The dicta of political economy on this matter have no validity whatever outside the assumption of the status of a commodity for labour and the industrial system based upon that assumption. They cease to apply the moment that status is questioned.

The Labour movement, in its century long struggle up to the unrest of the present day, is simply the record of the human revolt against the assumption of any such status for human beings. There can be no stable social order based upon the treatment of human life as a commodity in the market. To place living men and women in that relationship to society is to misinterpret human nature, its needs and desires and its inevitable movement towards their realization. The only possible stable relationship between human beings and society is a relationship which assumes them to be human beings, a relationship expressly directed to the satisfaction of their human needs, a relationship which regards the material resources of society as existing for no other purpose than the satisfaction of those needs. The instability of every social organization which universal history shows to have fallen ultimately into ruin can be traced to oversight of this primary law of human society, to the existence within that organization of human beings standing in a non-human relationship to society ; either destroying the organization by the pressure of their human claims against it by revolution from within, or weakening it into inability to resist attack from without.   To imagine that society can be permanently organized for the benefit of an owning class, and that the non-owning class can be catalogued with cotton and machinery and horses as a commodity, a supply of labour to be bought as may be necessary for the profit of the owning class, is the most credulous folly.   It was upon that foundation that the modern capitalist system began to erect its crazy structure, a foundation incompatible with the needs of human life. To prevent the structure from falling into immediate ruin, all sorts of buttresses and tie-rods and struts—all modern charity and philanthropy is that sort of prop-work for an order of society which denies elementary justice to its men and women—have had to be devised ; but in spite of soup kitchens and of social reform within the existing order, the whole thing is visibly crumbling into ruin. The craziness is an essential craziness in foundation. The stability of an organization of society depends upon its satisfaction of human needs ; and to begin by assuming human life to be a commodity is to begin by ignoring human nature and its needs altogether.

CHAPTER VI

THE GROWTH OF WORKING-CLASS CONSCIOUSNESS

THE revolt of human nature against the conditions of life imposed upon the nation by the industrial revolution came, in the first instance, and so far as it found expression in action, not from the workers themselves, but from sympathetic members of the governing classes.

It must be noted, in our survey of the position at the opening of this struggle a hundred years ago, that the working class had no political power, no direct control, or share of control, over national affairs. England possessed representative institutions, but they were class representative only. The day of political rights for the mass of the people had not yet dawned.

The passing of the first Factory Act in 1802, and the stirring of the national conscience which made that Act possible, was the work, mainly, of members of the governing class.

For it is not only inconsistent with human nature for men to suffer permanently a deprivation of human status amongst their fellows ; it is also inconsistent with human nature for men to endure seeing that deprivation inflicted upon their fellows. At all points the new capitalism, with its theory of labour as a commodity, mistook human nature in supposing that such a theory of the status of labour in human society could be made to wear in actual institutions.

But men are the slaves of habit, and the first instinct of those who revolted against the cruelties of the new industrial order was to fall back on tradition and on the past, instead of looking forward to a new synthesis which should adjust the new powers of wealth production to the needs of human life, and make society an ordered scheme of real human relationships on the higher level rendered possible by those new powers. Had they so looked forward, the solution of the difficulty would have been clear—national ownership of the tools and national organization of the new industry, as the only means, since the individual worker with his own tools was no longer possible, of uniting capitalist and labourer in one person and making the gains of the new industry available for the human

ife engaged in it.   But the time was not ripe
for that solution of the problem in citizenship.
The worker had still to win his citizenship, and
the State still had to be transformed from a
governing class to the nation acting co-opera-
tively.   The new synthesis of citizenship,
ultimately to be found the only solution of the
problem, was still remote ; and, though it
was all there in germ, there were many unfold-
ings and developments necessary before it
could take shape in men's minds.

The first instinct, therefore, of those who
saw the whole gain of the new industry being
diverted to ownership regardless of the human
interests engaged in it—the sudden growth of
bloated fortunes, like great tumours in the
national life, while the body of the people was
kept starved and sickly in order to feed these
accumulations of private wealth—their first
instinct was to get back to the old ideals and
to graft if possible the patriarchal virtues and
qualities of the feudal conception of life on
to the new capitalism.   They took for granted
the inevitability of private lordship over the
new wealth, and thought by moralizings
to turn it into a trusteeship ; that private
capitalism could be got to recognise human
claims, and to deal with men as men and not
merely as a commodity, a supply of labour

power to be bought in the cheapest market. A great deal of moralizing and preaching to capitalism on those lines, insistence upon wealth being regarded as a trusteeship, and so on, went on during that earlier period, with about as much effect upon the operations of capitalism as might have been expected if the same moralizings and preachings had been addressed to Vesuvius in eruption.

Very speedily it became evident that what could not be done by moral persuasion must be done, if it was to be done at all, by the compulsion of the law ; and so began the period of the first series of Factory Acts. We may take this period as extending from the passing of the elder Sir Robert Peel's Moral and Health Act in 1802 to Lord Althorp's Act of 1833. Carried in the face of the most furious opposition from the manufacturing interests, the series of Acts during this period did not even pretend to deal with the general question of the admitted evils of the new factory system. They were almost exclusively confined to dealing with some of the worst conditions of child labour. For at the outset of the new industrial régime, it was upon the child life of the country that the full force of the brutality of the system which regarded human beings as commodities fell most heavily.

The cheapest market for the human commodity
was the child market ; and the business of
buying child labour, working it at the highest
pressure, and replacing it with a fresh supply
as soon as it was worn out and killed by over-
work, disease, underfeeding, and being herded
under insanitary conditions, went on ruth-
essly.   Where the local supply of labour power
n children's bodies was insufficient, the manufacturers turned to the Poor Law for a fresh
supply of the commodity.   Before the advent
of steam power on any great scale, the factory
system developed most rapidly in such counties as Lancashire and Yorkshire, on account
of the abundance of water-courses and water
power ; and the supply of children in the district became inadequate.   The manufacturers
went accordingly to the more southern agricultural counties and cleared the parishes of
pauper children, transferring them to the new
factory districts, housing them in pent-up
buildings adjoining the factories, and working
them without intermission, " so that the beds
were said never to have become cold, inasmuch as one batch of children rested while
the other batch went to the looms, only half
the requisite number of beds being provided
for all."

From the point of view of the new capitalist

economics, there was nothing to complain about in all this. Labour was a commodity ; and the first law in the code of the new hell on earth was that nothing should be permitted to interfere with the buying of commodities in the cheapest market. It was on that definite and declared ground of economic principle that the manufacturing interests fought for all they were worth against the beginnings of factory legislation. But human nature, against which they had set up their economics, was too strong for them ; the conscience of the nation insisted upon regarding the children in some degree as human beings and not merely as commodities ; and so began the series of restrictions on child labour embodied in that early period of factory legislation.

The restrictions were trivial and in many cases ineffective at first. They still left the child-life of the factory districts a monstrous horror appealing to heaven against the commodity theory of human life. Compared with what we regard to-day as the minimum infringement permissible in the name of trade with the human rights of children, the restrictions imposed by these early Factory Acts were hardly worth noting. But they were of the greatest possible importance because they were the first legislative assertion of the new principle between which and the economics of capitalism the battle was ultimately to be fought out, the principle of regarding human life as human life and not as a commodity. Leaving details out of account, the issue between the two great fundamentally opposed views of human destiny, the human view and the commodity view, was defined in these first feeble beginnings.

At the outset, as we have noted, action came mainly from sympathetic persons of the governing class. It was not so much a labour revolt as a human nature revolt against a theory of life instinctively felt to be false by all good people. The mass of the people, rapidly degenerated under the influence of factory and slum life, were brutal, ignorant, hopeless and without vision. Their moral condition answered to their physical condition. Uneducated, shut out from the amenities of life, trained for no other human destiny than that of factory labour under filthy conditions, underfed and overdriven, character was rotted out of them ; and the human material of the nation was, under such conditions, inevitably besotted and rendered brutish to a very large degree, relaxing in its scanty non-working hours into the vicious, coarse, and dirty amusements of animality ; not at all because the human material was worse than human material in general, but because no chance of or access to training and opportunity and the knowledge of other things was within its reach.

But the human nature imprisoned in this filthy way of life was soon to give evidence of its existence. Under the measureless grossness and the slag nestled the seed of human desire for better things ; and with the Factory Act agitation originating with the more sympathetic members of the governing class it began to germinate. By the end of the first Factory Act period working class sentiment and working class agitation began to take the lead in these matters. The work of men like Richard Oastler, the Rev. Mr. Bull of Bradford, Thomas Sadler, and others, produced a great result in stirring working class opinion into active revolt ; and by the time that Lord Althorp's Act was passed there was a great and growing driving force of working class agitation behind the new movement. The movement, indeed, had never been without something of that driving force ; but the agitation over the Ten Hours Bill, preceding the Act of 1833, may be taken as the definite assumption of the lead in the struggle by working class opinion itself.

Thenceforth and throughout the century, with growing insistence and with a vision steadily clearing as to the real character of the issue, the record becomes more and more the definite record of class war.

The slow progress made in Factory legislation, the ability of the manufacturing interest to thwart and cut down such legislation by reason of their increasing hold upon political power, and the miserably small improvement in actual life visible as a result of what was being done on these lines, all this had its inevitable moral result in awakening the wage-earning class to a beginning of class consciousness. The outrages inflicted upon human life, and the inability of legislation largely controlled by the manufacturing interests to do more than give the most trifling alleviation, and that only after hard and prolonged agitation utterly disproportionate to the results, led inevitably to the next stage in the development. Under the irritation of that slow progress, disturbances and disorders broke out incessantly, the incoherent expression of the anger of men who felt that their way of life was unjust and intolerable, and that organized society was being of no material help to them in their struggle against the injustice. And, as always happens when such incoherent manifestations of finding life intolerable take place, a coherent and definite purpose began to appear in the midst of the confusion.

This coherent and definite purpose was in the realization by the working class that, instead of appealing to others, they must secure justice for themselves, must win their own right to human life if it was to be won at all. What is the use of appealing to organized society? they asked themselves. We have no voice or vote in organized society. Instead of asking other people, and they the very people whose interests are opposed to ours, to make laws for our benefit, we must fight our way into citizenship and the right to a direct voice in making laws for ourselves.

The movement for the realization of this new definite purpose in the development of the labour revolt against the inhuman conditions of life took two forms—the growth of trade unionism, and the pressure for political rights and enfranchisement into citizenship.

And with those developments we reach the real beginning of the struggle leading directly to the Labour Unrest of to-day and all that it implies in our national life ; for what these

G

developments did was to set up definitely the claim of the worker, not only to human life, but to human life out of patriarchal leading strings, to human life on the footing of self-governing citizenship.

CHAPTER VII

TRADE UNIONISM

Of these two developments, let us first consider the part played by trade unionism in the wide-sweeping movement of the nineteenth century towards the economic freedom of the workers and their deliverance from the status of a commodity to the human status of citizens engaged in the production and distribution of wealth for their own human advantage and endowment.

Although, as civilization is now beginning to see, that is the destined purpose of the whole movement, the end to which all these contributory factors are now visibly drawing together, no such comprehensive purpose entered the mind of trade unionism at its inception. As we noted at the outset, the increasing purpose which runs through an age is never discerned in its comprehensiveness until it draws so near its completion as to be unmistakable. The early trade unionists had not the slightest idea that their movement was

a stage in the development of the attack upon
the private capitalist system of conducting
the industry of the nation.   They were merely
taking steps to protect themselves by union
against some of the more crushing and unbear-
able detailed injustices under which they
suffered.   A little better treatment here and
a petty improvement there—that was the
limit of their vision and their immediate aim.
Social reorganization and the conception of
the co-operative commonwealth never entered
their heads at all.

But, none the less, trade unionism played its
part in, and made its invaluable contribution
to, the greater movement of economic emancipation of which the world now begins to
discern the significance.   Its immediate ac-
complishments mattered little or nothing.
Whether it secured a little more or a little
less by pressure here or by a strike there is
quite unimportant.   The real part which it
had to play was in bringing about in the minds
of the workers a gradual realization of certain
fundamental truths which had to be recognized
before the purpose of the wider movement
could become a conscious and adopted purpose.
The immediate programme of reforms which
it set out to accomplish was trivial and
detailed, and wholly within the existing

order ; but its immense value at this stage in the development of affairs was that it formulated, not a programme, but a frame of mind, an attitude towards society on the part of the workers.

What trade unionism did in this respect was to give recognition to the definite and direct conflict of interest between classes. It was a form of class organization which implicitly, even though it was generally unconscious of the implication, admitted the existence of class war. It defined an antagonism, and, by the very nature of its activities, represented the employing class to the mind of the worker as an enemy against whose aggressions it was necessary to act in class combination if one was to act effectually. By the very fact of its existence it implied opposition, resistance, the presence of an adversary, a contest of interests in the distribution of wealth. It was the expression of the fact that class was against class in the distribution of the products of industry ; and it had no reason for existence except as such an expression. As an organization for defence, it implied the existence of an attack against which protection was necessary. Slowly but surely it accustomed working-men to think of their class interests as interests subject to steady and constant attack, unless they were constantly on the alert to defend them. It put the relationship between classes into an atmosphere of conflict, and habituated the wage-earner to that way of regarding class distinctions. It was a standing denial to the suggestion that the interests of the capitalist class and of the wage-earner are identical. Every man who joined a trade union did so because he knew that his interests were not identical with those of his master, and that there would be no reason for his joining a trade union if they were ; that his master's interest was to get his labour as cheaply as possible, while his own interest was to get as decent a human life as he could out of the sale of his labour. To the employing class labour was a commodity, and the less expensive it was the better. To the workman labour was human life, and cheap labour meant insufficient food, leaky boots for the children, scanty household comforts for the family. Trade unionism was the instinctive recognition by the workers that here was no identity of interest, but conflict and antagonism ; and it was the formulation of this antagonism into the habitual mood of working-class life that trade unionism was mainly responsible for bringing about.

But its immediate aims were merely detailed

aims within the existing order of society. It saw no further than the constant need for alertness in what it took for granted to be a permanent antagonism between classes. The idea of ending the conflict by merging the classes into a nation on a footing of common interests was remote from it. Evils are felt before their causes are discerned or their nature understood. Trade unionism, though a coherent movement in relation to the previous unorganized condition of the working-classes, was still incoherent in relation to the larger purpose which it was none the less helping to bring to birth in the consciousness of the nation. It felt the evil, but neither discerned its cause nor fully understood its nature, and therefore organized itself for momentary purposes of resistance only.

This recognition of the fact of a fundamental conflict of interest between classes was the primary contribution of trade unionism to the increasing realization by the age of the larger purpose to which the facts of life had committed it—committed it as yet unconsciously but none the less completely. And, side by side with that, or, to speak more accurately, bound up with it, was some degree of discernment of the nature of the conflict. Just as the recognition of the fact

of conflict was implicit in the very existence of trade unionism, so the beginning of
discernment of the nature of the conflict was
implicit in the aims of trade unionism, even
in its trivial detailed aims.   From the outset,
it was waged as a conflict between the commodity view of human life and the flesh-and-
blood view.   As we have seen, labour was to
the employing class only a commodity to be
bought in the cheapest market.   To trade
unionism, even in its most trumpery pursuit of
a slight improvement here or there, labour was
always and essentially human life pressing its
human claims against the capitalist definition
of its status as a commodity.   Here, embodied
in all sorts of trifling demands and narrowly
limited conceptions of the claims of human
life, was nevertheless the primary antagonism,
an understanding of which is the master-key
to the history of civilization since the coming
of the machine industry.

Once such a class organization of revolt is
set going, based upon such fundamental
principles as these, it grows steadily and
irresistibly towards a fuller and more comprehensive view of the significance of its
own underlying principles of action and of
organization.   Its limited view at the outset
matters nothing so long as the essential idea

is there ; its due development and unfolding
is only a matter of time and of the provocation
which circumstances bring to bear upon its
growth. It was in the nature of things that
its full significance should be hidden at the
outset. Men do not spring into so large a
comprehension all in a moment ; and the
period of growth and provocation brings
another quality into the movement as necessary to the final attainment as comprehension
is, the quality of the revolutionary temper as
well as of a rational understanding. It is
not sufficient for men to see economic processes
clearly. There must be the driving force
also. The driving force of a revolutionary
temper without clear knowledge and constructive aims intelligently understood leads
to mere disorder and chaos ; but on the other
hand the most perfect understanding of
economic processes leads of itself to no action
at all, for action has its origin in desire and
the fervour for an attainment. And in the
long period of trade union struggle this
essential quality has grown in strength and
intensity side by side with the growth of
understanding, a moral force without which
the impetus for the final phases of the struggle
would have been wanting. Although for the
moment spending itself in detail within the

existing order, trade unionism, in its incessant conflicts with the commodity view of human labour, has given this quality to the economic revolution. Its defeats and exasperations, no less than its successes and its apparent attainments, have all been effective to this end ; often, indeed, more effective. And with this persistent development of the revolutionary temper has come the clearer understanding. Defeats have invariably been followed by a greater and more abiding sense of the need for class solidarity and an increasing perception of the fundamental conflict of interests. Nothing was wasted in this stage of the struggle ; nothing, however apparently futile at the moment, was without its due effect in the training of the disinherited class, training in respect of both temperament and knowledge, for the revolutionary task awaiting them.

Looking back from the standpoint of to-day upon that earlier history of trade unionism, we see this growing class cohesion and widening conception of the function of the movement. We see the intelligently directed purpose begin to appear in it, more and more clearly visible in successive struggle after struggle ; growing thoroughness of aim, and a steady development out of the stage of formless and exasperated revolt against immediate grievances into the stage of definite purposes more and more related to the primary issue of the status of the worker in the nation, and his economic relationship to society.

CHAPTER VIII

THE POLITICAL REVOLUTION

THIS growth within the labour movement of definite purposes directly related to the status of the worker in society instead of being limited to minor issues of detail within his existing status, took in the first instance a political rather than an economic direction; and manifested itself in the steady development of the claim to political enfranchisement. The capture of political power, the attainment of a status of effective citizenship, became the urgent matter for labour.

It was in the natural order of precedence in development that, in the working out of the new synthesis of democracy as a form of social organization, the political aspect of democracy should come before its economic aspect; and should take possession of men's minds as a complete synthesis of organized society before its character as a complete economic synthesis also was even suspected. By democracy men meant simply the extension

of political rights to all, and the conception
of democracy was limited to its political forms.
The political rights and powers to be attained
by the people would, it was taken for granted,
be used to remedy social and industrial injustices; but the conception of what democracy
meant on that side was still vague and undefined, and strictly limited to the possibility
of detailed reforms within the existing order.
That democracy was an economic as well as
a political philosophy of social organization,
a philosophy as clear and definite in its bearing
upon industrial forms as upon political forms,
and that the new social synthesis involved in
the democratic idea was incomplete until its
economic implications were seen as clearly
as were its political implications, was still
hidden from men's minds. Naturally so;
for only an experience of citizenship in actual
operation could teach men that lesson. It is
in the very nature of human action that men
only see their immediate task before them,
and only discover its implications, the in-
completeness of its attainment, by experience
of the facts of life. That democracy was a
life to be lived, and a political form only in so
far as that kind of life required a method of
political organization adjusted to its service;
and that the political form in itself was no

more complete democracy than a knife and
fork is a dinner, was only to become clear in
time.

But although, in the struggle for political
rights, only the half of democracy was clearly
seen, and that the lesser half, the clothes and
accoutrements rather than the actual reality
of democracy, nevertheless the attainment of
political rights was discerned synthetically.
Those who advocated political democracy were
not merely pottering about with detailed
reforms within the existing order. They saw
life as a whole, and could express their purposes, what they were doing and where they
were going, in the large language of a definite
scheme, a philosophy of political forms. It
was not a reform movement, but a revolutionary movement ; having for its purpose the
definite substitution of one order of society
for another, the transformation of the community from the class-divided condition of
governors and governed to the classless condition of a self-governing citizenship within
which all men should stand on a footing of
equality with regard to the possession and
exercise of political rights. That the attainment was gradual, that the franchise was
spread by degrees over a constantly enlarging
proportion of the population, that it continued

to be held unequally in such survivals as plural
voting, that its powers were limited by the
existence of an hereditary and non-representative element in the Constitution, and by the
vast grinning mediæval absurdity of the
procedure of the House of Commons ; all this
in no way invalidates the conception of
democracy as self-governing citizenship exercised in equality by all members of the community.   For every one knows that whatever
there may be in our political forms inconsistent
with the equality of self-governing citizenship
is doomed ; that the battle for the principle
has been won ; and that although a year or a
decade seems a long time to the people who
live through it, in the perspective of history
the establishment of self-governing citizenship exercised in equality, and the elimination
of such elements of inequality as have sur-
vived for a short time into the new political
order, will be seen as one single co-ordinated
and rather brief revolutionary transaction.
We see our own years and decades in a very
much more extended and prolonged way than
history will see them ; and if a proposal for
legislation has to be postponed for a couple
of Parliamentary sessions, we begin to feel that
continuity on the line of that legislation has
suffered a severe check.   We fret for small

completions and see them in fragmentary
detail ; whereas history notes the process as
a whole and brings it within the compass of
a glance.   So it is with the political revolution.
From the moment that the conception of
democracy in political forms took synthetic
shape in men's minds, and began to realize
itself in institutions as the working out of a
definite principle to a definite end, the
defence of these survivals of privilege and
inequality has ceased to be a defence on
principle, and has become only a temporary
expedient of delay ; the length of their sur-
vival being dependent upon the degree to
which they remain quiescent and are not
used aggressively against the new order of
things.   To resurrect them into effective use
is to bring about their extinction.   The recent
story of the House of Lords and the present
position with regard to plural voting make
that very clear.

The first and immediate consequence of the
beginning of the conquest of political power
by the working classes was the discovery of
the need for education.   " We must educate
our masters."   It was seen at once to be a
grave danger to the State if the control of its
affairs should be put into the hands of uneducated men, untrained for rational and in-

telligent judgment on national issues. Here
again was a new revolutionary factor intro-
duced into the general movement of the
national life. As with the spread of the
franchise, so with the spread of facilities for
education ; the thing began in a small way
with strictly limited elementary education,
and a very low school age. But once such a
force is set free to work in society, its growth
and expansion are irresistible. There is now
seen to be no stopping short of educational
equality any more than there can be a stopping
short of political equality. The improvement
of elementary education and the raising of the
school age followed rapidly upon the first
introduction of public education ; and as
soon as the public schools began to turn out a
generation of young people who could read
and study, a generation to whom literature
and science were accessible, the pressure for
further facilities resulted in a constant raising
of the standard, and finally in the extension of
public provision from elementary to se-
condary and higher education. There is
no need to pursue the point. Whatever may
be the delays and the stages of attainment,
every one now knows perfectly well that
educational equality is assured, that the
battle for the principle has been won, and

that class privilege is on the way to becoming obsolete in this respect as completely as in respect of political power.

All this is contained in democracy from the very outset. Given the idea of democracy, and these things come of it by inevitable development.

And is not the further implication of economic equality there also ?

Given a community of educated men possessing political power, with a sense of economic injustice pressing heavily upon them, and round about them in society the spectacle of the growth of wealth and ostentation out of the product of their own industry ; and is the end in any sort of doubt whatever ?

They may begin their struggle for political power with only the vaguest and most indefinite notion of what they will do with it when they get it. But they feel instinctively that the possession of political power should be effective in securing a betterment in their industrial position. That was the mood in which the English labour movement set out for the attainment of political rights. The immediate economic purpose seen in it was only the setting right of certain explicit detailed grievances ; but over and above all that was the general feeling of living in an atmosphere of injustice. " This cramped life, this constant penury in the midst of wealth, is not right, not just. I do not know what it may be, but I am being badly hurt all my days. My children have no prospect but drudgery. My status is a status of drudgery. I resent it ; something is wrong somewhere in the ordering of affairs."

That is a revolutionary mood, a revolutionary temper.

Given education, the diffusion of intelligence and the possession of political power, on the top of that mood and temper, and human economic equality must inevitably come of it. Once such forces are set going, the existence of a permanently disinherited class in society becomes unthinkable. Government so controlled must tend, steadily and with increasing directness of aim, to become government in the interest of the whole community and not in the interest of a class only. The society in which an educated democracy possess political power cannot continue to be a society organized industrially for the advantage of a comparatively small possessing class, or to keep any of its human constituents in the status of a commodity. The idea of government in such a nation must inevitably expand so as to cover the economic

; well as the political organization of
)ciety

For the disabilities under which men feel
ley suffer in actual life are the economic
isabilities. It is in that region the injustice
es. Political disabilities are not felt, and
ould pass unnoticed, unless there is discom-
)rt and a sense of deprivation in actual life.
: is in the very nature of democracy that a
)cial order politically controlled by the whole
eople should work with the inevitability of
ravitation towards a common standard of
eneral welfare, and should compel its in-
ustrial organization to conform to that end.

The conditions set up by political demo-
racy and by the spread of education are,
ierefore, a sure prophecy of the attainment
f such an economic basis of society as will
erve the interests of the whole people as
pposed to class privilege and sectional in-
erests pursued at the expense of the rest of
ie community. Political democracy com-
iits us to that. The thing is as good as
one, in its absolute certainty as the outcome
f political democracy. There is no meaning
r purpose or sanity in political democracy
kcept in that development ; and those who
ght for political democracy and for education
re, whether they are conscious of it or not,

only the pioneers of social democracy, engaged in the preliminary work of clearing the ground and setting up the scaffolding for the erection of the real democratic structure of society in economics and industry and the actual facts of life and work.

That, then, was the process of development upon which the labour movement entered when it began to concentrate upon the attainment of political rights. It was to discover by experience that the rights which it believed to be final and conclusive were only a preliminary and preparatory equipment for the real work of emancipation ; but for the moment, and necessarily so, the attainment of that equipment seemed all in all.

CHAPTER IX

THE ADVENT OF THE LABOUR PARTY

ııs development brings us close up to our
ʌn time.

What had been gained in the struggle so
r ?

So far as the essential economic relationship
the working population to society was con-
rned, nothing. That relationship remained
ıtouched. The curtain which rose at the
ıening of the industrial drama upon a work-
g population separated from the ownership
the means of its work, with no footing of
ſ own in the national life, with no human
ıtus in industry, but only the status of a
mmodity to be bought as cheaply as
ıssible by the rulers of industry, for whose
le benefit wealth production was carried
ı, and who alone constituted organized
ciety in their appropriation of the benefits
civilization and of the increased pro-
ıctivity of industry, fell again after a first
t which left that essential relationship

between classes unchanged. A few of the excesses of private ownership had been checked. The child life of the nation has been to some extent withdrawn from the labour-commodity market, and remained up to a certain age underfed at home instead of being underfed and worked to death in the factory. It still remained, of course, involved in the struggle, through its class associations and the government of its home conditions by the fact that its parent continued to be a commodity, a thing for sale in the cheapest market, instead of a human being sharing in the national resources. The economic relationship of the worker to society was in all its essentials as before ; and the first act passed, so far as the economic conditions were concerned, in a series of small movements for small modifications having no bearing upon that essential relationship, any more than proposals for reducing the number of lashes which a slave-owner might inflict upon his slaves touched the essential fact of their slavery

But, notwithstanding that, the action of the drama had moved and developed during that first act. Whereas the curtain rose upon a working population having neither an economic nor a political status in the nation, a working population disorganized and without

onsciousness of its position, with only a
lind sense of injustice stirring it to occasional
haotic disorders and evidences of resentment,
t fell upon a working population with a class
onsciousness, a working population consolida-
ing into trade unions, definite class organiza-
ions for defence and aggression, engaged in
he definite constructive purpose of capturing
oolitical power and securing its status in
:itizenship.

Upon that position the second act opens ;
apon a working-class population equipped
vith the beginnings of political power, of
education, and a sense of class solidarity.
Feeble, limited, immature beginnings, no
loubt, but with all the potency and assurance of growth, all the certainty of maturity
and of ultimate direction towards the economic
evolution of which they were the necessary
oolitical preliminaries.

And so we come to the fascinating chapter
ecording the progress of political democracy
n the working out of the industrial revolution,
vith its initial limitations steadily widening,
ts strength coming to it through futile experi-
nent after futile experiment, each leading to
lew endeavour on broader lines and with firmer
;rasp of the facts of life ; learning by its errors,
narching down by-paths to dead-ends of no

attainment, and back again to the main road with one more possibility of error known and avoided for the future ; the whole movement going on so rapidly and vigorously that a single generation can survey the facts within its own experience.

The primary lesson which experience had to hammer into the consciousness of the working class after their attainment of political rights was that political democracy of itself does not in the least interfere with the rule of the rich, with servility, with subjection in actual life to the owners of the means of the world's work. Political democracy, which many men, in the fervour of fighting for it, had come to regard as an end in itself, had to be discovered as only a means to an end. The fact that men with votes could starve, be sweated and overworked, remain mere commodities in the labour market, with just as much discomfort and under just as much deprivation as men without votes, until such time as they were intelligent enough to use their votes for the control of their economic conditions, might seem so obvious as to need no demonstration by experience, and to be one of the axioms of political endeavour from the outset.

But it was not so. While, no doubt, there was a dim realization of the fact that political

franchisement would lead to social and
dustrial betterment, there was a tendency
the outset to leave the thing to work itself
t automatically.   The newly enfranchised
orking population came into its citizenship
t as a new, separate, self-contained organiza-
on of the political life of the nation.   The
d political parties, existing amongst the class
hich had previously had exclusive possession
political power, held the field and covered
e whole range of political organization, with
eir governing families, their Parliamentary
ocedure, their traditional way of carrying
the business of the nation.   And the new
orking-class electorate began by simply
taching itself to one or other of these parties.
had no conception of itself as a governing
wer, as the new nation, as a competitor with
e parties representing the old order for
e control of national affairs.   It accepted
eir rule, their party organization, their
verning families, and their procedure;
d relied at the outset upon the hope that the
ct of its presence in the electorate would
ve a colour and a tendency to the action of
e governing parties more helpful and sym-
athetic to labour than had been the case
eviously.   And it largely stultified even
ch influence as it might have exercised in

that way by dividing its electoral support indifferently between the two parties of the old State.

This process of absorption into the old political parties was facilitated by the way in which the franchise was extended in instalments. The admission of the working class to political rights was a piecemeal admission—a group here and a group there, town workers by one Act, agricultural workers by another—and under such conditions as to continuous residence, separate house occupation, and the like, that large numbers, nominally enfranchised, were in any year liable to be disfranchised by having, for example, to remove from one district to another in following their employment, and so on. With no political experience in the working of electoral machinery, it was not unnatural that the new groups of electors, coming into citizenship in separate detachments in this way, and with a good deal of uncertainty in their continuous tenure of the vote from year to year, should fall under the influence of the powerful party organizations which, between them, divided the control of political life and of the electoral machinery of the nation. The new electorate were not called in to start a new concern, but to take part in a going concern ; and it would have been

inconsistent with the limitations of human
conduct to expect them to have set about at
once to have devised new electoral machinery
and a new party organization of their own.
They had not the cohesion for that. Their
feeling of class solidarity, although growing
vigorously, was still too immature to make
any such initiative possible. It was finding
expression in their trade unionism; but the
time was not yet ripe for its extension to
political organization. The tradition that to
be a politician was to be either a Liberal or
a Conservative was unquestioned; and the
new electors, born alive into the world of
political rights, like the boys and girls in
Gilbert's song, had to be one or the other if
they were to be in the political swim at all.
There was no way at the moment of exer-
cising their new political rights at all, except
through the medium of the existing parties
which chose the candidates, financed the
electoral business, and conducted the whole
of the arrangements. It was not by any
means apathy that led to the absorption of
the workers in the old parties, but simply
the impossibility, under the circumstances,
of finding an expression for one's political
activities outside these two political groups
in possession of the whole political machinery.

The relief of the propertied classes at this development was great. Many of them had figured to themselves the enfranchisement of the working classes as the letting loose of a new political force which would sweep away old landmarks and supersede their governing order ; and the spectacle of the new electorate being quietly absorbed in the old parties, without any apparent real effect on the continuity of the rule of the old governing families, was most comforting. Certain slight concessions were necessary, no doubt. You had to keep these fellows in hand now that they had votes ; but it was a wonderful tribute to the sound practical common sense of working men to see how little really was necessary to that end. Election phrases specially addressed to them, a little more diligence in meeting them at public gatherings, being nice to their women-folk, and all that sort of thing, was found to be sufficient in many cases. It was really quite touching to see how that sympathetic manner towards them—out of which you could get a good deal of genuine sport at election time to set against the nuisance of it—induced them to throw up their caps for you and cheer your return as though it were the fulfilment of the prophecies. But as for serious politics—well, it was satisfactory to see that they knew their place, and were content to leave that to you; to regard the politician of the old parties as a superior person with a destiny for governing, and themselves as voting items hopefully expectant of such slight favours as the mystery and difficulty of State affairs—in which superstition of mystery and difficulty it was your main business in your speeches to keep them—permitted you to bestow upon them. Meanwhile, the old order, the old rule, the old political dynasties and sham fights, went on very comfortably.

And so also went on very comfortably the real ruling of the country as distinguished from the sham political rule—the real rule of the masters of the nation's bread in the actual daily life and work of the people, the economic rule and government of private ownership over industry, with labour as a commodity in the market. The attainment of political rights was very speedily found to be having no effect upon that. The bread-and-butter problems which the worker had to face daily in his family affairs, the deprivations which he and his wife and children suffered in the midst of abounding and increasing wealth, his own bare sustenance out of the national resources compared with the ever-rising scale of social ostentation and luxury which his masters were getting out of the new powers of wealth production—the rancour and the sense of injustice of all this remained with him. And his vote did not seem to be helping him to any extent worth mentioning.

Political democracy, realizing that fact, realizing it with increasing clearness and force, began again feeling its way through a further series of futile experiments. It was still seeking for nothing more than social reforms within the existing order ; and its discontent was with the slowness of the pace rather than with the direction of such reforms. Its electoral influence was proving of little or no effect, compared with the felt needs of working class life ; and it set itself to quicken the pace.

Detachment from tradition is always a difficult business ; and for a considerable period the effort to quicken the pace was on the line of the old tradition of the existing political parties, bringing increasing working-class pressure for reforms to bear within the old parties upon candidates of the old type. The party machinery still worked to the old governing class idea in its selection of candidates and its notion of Parliamentary representatives as superior persons of the governing

rder ; but although the pressure from below
iad not yet got to the point of throwing off
he governing-class idea in that respect, it
;howed a steadily increasing intention of
naking such representatives amenable to the
views of the new electorate in matters affecting
vorking-class life.

The awakening political consciousness of
he working-class electorate throughout this
)hase of the development can only be under-
;tood by the constant reference of the results
ittained by legislation back to the facts of
ife. Men with actual grievances cannot be
'obbed off for ever with rhetoric and with
)erorations. What have I gained ? Am I
iny forwarder ? Are the conditions of my
laily life and work substantially improved ?
The constant reference of legislation back to
hat test, bringing the rhetoric and the perora-
ions face to face with reality, is the most
:ducational of all processes when exercised
)y men possessing political power. They
ooked at their gains and found them trifling.
)aily experience rubbed in the lesson. The
acts of life, the facts with which they worked
nd ate and slept, the real presence of misery
nd discomfort in working-class existence—
hese were their constant daily reminders of
he futility of their political powers. The

little improvements here and there to which the politicians pointed in their speeches as evidence of progress and as reasons for retaining the confidence of working-class electors could not stand that test. They left the main facts of poverty as before.

The failure was at first attributed to the unsympathetic character of political representation. When working-class electors noted the fact that the Liberal or the Conservative candidate for whom they had voted at the last election was the capitalist against whom, a little later, they were out on strike for better conditions, they began to wonder whether, after all, the representation of working men by employers in Parliament was of any particular service to them. They began to ask themselves whether it was reasonable to expect that, by using their political power to place members of the employer and land-owning classes in Parliament, they were likely to get working-class reforms, dealing with the same questions over which they had to fight these same persons in their non-political character as employers. Was the employer one man and the politician another man in the same skin ? Was the railway director who fought them from the board-room likely to legislate in their interests when they returned him to

I

Parliament as a Liberal or a Conservative? On the whole, it began to be perceived that the choice between Liberals and Conservatives while candidatures were still monopolised by the rich class, was really no choice at all ; or, at most, a choice between whether one would wish to be afflicted with a hump or with a squint ; and that whether a Liberal employer or a Conservative employer was returned, he remained an employer, with an employer's class interests.

And so appeared the movement for Labour representation. Here again, as throughout the whole development, the new idea found its first expression in such a form as to break away as little as possible from the old tradition. The movement for Labour representation was at first a movement within the existing parties—chiefly the Liberal party, as having been mainly responsible for political enfranchisement.

It is customary nowadays, from the standpoint of later developments, to speak in terms of utter derision of the Lib-Lab chapter in the story of Labour representation. That is a very unfair way of treating it. From the point of view of any impression which it actually made upon the poverty problem, of its accomplishment in altering, or even getting within sight of, the essential relationship of subjection in which the wage-earner stood to the masters of the nation's industry, it was no doubt, contemptible enough. Under the growing pressure of working-class opinion, a small corner of the Liberal benches in the House of Commons was consecrated to the accommodation of a few actual working-men; and when one of them was exalted to the dizzy eminence of an under-secretaryship, one might almost have thought, from the official Liberal glorification of its own action in making that great promotion, that all the hopes and aspirations of working-men were fulfilled in such a consummation. But to treat the Lib-Lab episode with derision would be as unfair and ungenerous as for a grown man in his strength to regard with contempt the crawlings and tumblings of his infancy by which he gathered strength and prepared for the vigour of maturity. Liberal-Labour representation was a necessary stage in the growth of political class consciousness amongst the disinherited. The fact that Liberalism consented to it was in itself evidence of the increasing pressure from below; and the appearance of this group in the House of Commons, powerless as its members were, except in the merest detail, against the forces of wealth which dominated not only the House of Commons but also their own party, was a conspicuous landmark on the road which the workers had to travel to their emancipation.

This phase was a very brief one. The very fact that an entry had been forced into the House of Commons, even though on such a footing, showed that the determination of the wage-earning class to make their political power a reality had so far developed as to make swifter and larger movement possible. It was a sign of gathering impetus, of the consolidation of forces capable of a more rapid and powerful advance. There was always that reference of attainment back to the facts of life ; and with the growing class-consciousness of working-class electors the application of that test became steadily swifter and more incisive ; the detection of futility in results, in their bearing on the actual facts of poverty and disinheritance, more immediate and assured.

All this, as we have seen, was only the natural development of the democratic idea. Given the possession of political power and the spread of intelligence, and democracy not only works inevitably towards an equalization of status and advantages amongst all citizens,

but works with constantly accelerating movement.   Futile experiments have a briefer and
briefer run ; the test of actual life conditions
becomes more imperative and more urgent.

And so the futility of Labour representation
within the old parties controlled by the owner
and master class, its failure to make any real
impression on the facts of life, became very
speedily apparent.   And, with a swiftness that
took the nation's breath away, there arose a
new movement—the movement for Independent Labour Representation.

Here at last, through a process of continuous
development, easily seen in retrospect to
have been all involved in the very beginnings
of political democracy, was the attainment of
a complete synthetic conception of political
rights by the working class.   They began their
career of political enfranchisement as voting
cattle, heads to be counted in summing up
the political influence of this or that group of
old governing families in the State, owned
politically as they were owned economically
by the master class, voting on issues raised
and defined by the master class in politics to
the constant exclusion of the real issues bearing upon the essential antagonism between
classes, and hoping for little more than a
slightly increased sympathetic consideration

of their needs by their masters in politics as a result of the competition for their votes between this and that party. Under the driving force of the facts of life and a continuing sense of injustice remaining unremedied, their grasp of the meaning, the promise and the potency of their political power, grew and grew from its infancy in pressure brought increasingly to bear upon the old parties to its claim for direct expression in representation within the old parties, testing the worth of the results attained at every stage by experience ; moving rapidly, by the abandonment of one proved futility after another, to the final stage of setting up their own complete, self-contained, self-controlled means of political expression ; coming in upon sufferance or as voting appendages to their masters no longer, but realizing themselves as the new nation, with the purpose, clearly seen at last, of governing in their own right and by their own power as masters in the State. And so rapid was the development that the first intimation which many people had of its existence was the appearance of a new Labour Party thirty strong in the House of Commons at the election of 1906.

CHAPTER X

THE alarm created amongst the proprietary classes by that first dramatic appearance of the new Labour Party in force in the House of Commons will be within everybody's recollection. The newspapers broke out into hysteria about menaced civilization, and bewildered politicians of the old parties talked about the impending end of all things.

And then came the pause, the watching for revolutionary events which did not happen ; and the gradual return of ease and confidence again, with the Labour Party an accepted factor in the normal political life of the country, and the exploitation of the workers in actual industrial life going on as usual.

The workers had found their political expression. They had learned how to exercise their political power. They had yet to learn their economic lesson as to the purpose for which that power was to be exercised. They had discerned democracy as a political synthesis only, with dimly seen possibilities of undefined social reform contained in it. They had yet to discover the economic synthesis of democracy, which would give to those dimly seen possibilities the form and order of a definite purpose—the meaning of democracy in the industrial relationship of the worker to society. And they had to arrive at a conception of that economic synthesis by a process of experience as inevitable as that by which they had attained to their synthetic conception of political democracy.

So far, although the pressure towards the attainment of political power had its origin in the economic and industrial conditions of life, it had been pressure due to dissatisfaction with the pace of social reform rather than with the direction of economic change. The economic outlook was confined to social reform within the existing order; and no synthetic quality of thought, bearing upon the essential economic relationship of the worker to society, was as yet generally apparent in the movement. The very active and aggressive beginnings of such a quality were evident enough, so evident, indeed, that the task of bringing the political class consciousness of the workers to the point of actual expression in independent Labour Party re-

presentation had been mainly carried through
by the influence of men identified with the
Socialist organizations ; but the general movement was still so far lacking in any such
quality that many of its adherents only
regarded themselves as advanced Radicals,
while a considerable proportion of seats secured by the party at its first onset were
secured in double-member constituencies with
the assistance of the practically solid Liberal
vote given in return for Labour votes to the
Liberal candidate, with whom the representation of the constituency was in that way
divided. The thought of the new party on
economic questions was still, for the most
part, entangled with the existing order.
And having attained political expression in
that fashion, the Labour Party set itself to
work empirically for such detached social
reforms as seemed to be most urgent at the
moment. It had to find its own economic
soul by the same process of futile experiment
after futile experiment, leading constantly
nearer to the economic synthesis of democracy, as had been necessary for the attainment of its complete political vision.

But the process was to be very much
briefer. Many confusions had already been
cleared up in the course of the political

struggle ; and that struggle had not been without its effect upon the development of economic vision. Education was more widespread than in the corresponding early stages of the political development ; a considerable force of synthetic thought on the economic aspect of democracy was present from the outset in the new party ; and the disposition to look for essential things and to define first principles, as against the empirical quackery of seeing nothing but a confusion of separate detailed reforms, was already strong within the party at its inception. Strong, but not dominant ; not yet sufficient to save the party from that by-path of social reform within the existing order which, it was to discover by experiment, led to no satisfaction for the economic needs of the worker. And therefore it was down that apparently promising by-path that the new party plunged its Parliamentary way, dragging with it, to their manifest discomfort and against their better judgment, those men in it who had a sufficient synthetic vision to know that the army must sooner or later march back again to the main revolutionary road of advance before becoming an effective force for the emancipation of industry.

It was unavoidable, under the circumstances, that it should be so. It was a great accomplishment to have got such a party into being at all; the organized expression of the political class consciousness of the workers. It would probably not have come into being without considerable further delay had the attempt been made to constitute it on a basis of economic principles as yet outside the general working-class consciousness. It came together simply as an expression of political class consciousness; and it had to learn its economics in the only way in which they could be learnt, by experience of the futility of the economic empiricism with which it started out. Meanwhile it was an enormous gain to have got it actually in being and at work.

Its advent had an immediate effect upon the old political parties. It aimed at quickening the pace in social reform; and it certainly succeeded. Alarmed beyond measure at the threatened loss of working class confidence and working class votes, of which the appearance of the new party was so substantial an expression, the old parties, which had delayed and delayed social reform for a generation, yielding nothing except to pressure, and then only in such measured driblets as they calculated would be just sufficient to ward

off violent public disorders, broke out into a
perfect frenzy of affection for the worker,
and desire to serve him with the social reforms
upon which he was insisting in so unpleasantly
threatening a manner. " My dear friend,"
you can hear them saying, " my very dear
friend, we had no idea, really, no idea at all,
that you wanted it so badly. Social reform ?
By all means, by all means. Take old-age
pensions. Take the feeding of necessitous
school children. Take labour bureaux. Take
small holdings. Take insurance against sick-
ness and unemployment. If you don't see
what you want in the window, come right in
and ask for it." All these things, a perfect
coruscation of social reform fireworks, marked
the period of six years following upon the
advent of the Labour Party as a period of
more abundant social reform legislation than
the sixty years previous. Nor has one party
been behind the other in its enthusiasm for
this legislation. It has for the most part been
passed by the general consent of the House ;
and Conservative members have been able to
recover damages for libel against any person
base enough to suggest that they were hostile
to old-age pensions or to the feeding of school
children. Assuredly, so far as quickening the
pace in social reform legislation is concerned,

the Labour Party could claim to have been most completely successful.

So successful, indeed, that they were lost sight of in their success. All at once, every party in the State had become eager for a quickening of the pace in social reform legislation, and the Labour Party, so far as that line of action was concerned, were lost in the crowd ; and the man in the street became unable to distinguish them from any other section of supporters of the Government in office.

The very fact of the immediate response of the old parties to the Labour Party demand for a quickening of the pace in social legislation, might have warned the party that it was wandering down a by-path. Marching down that alluring road with flags waving and drums beating for the attack on class privilege, it found itself received, not with hostility, but with open arms ; banquets spread for it, and a daily garland placed upon its head by all the Government newspapers for its statesmanship, its practical business acumen, its respectability, and above all its level-headed freedom from wild revolutionary ideas. It was an astonishing reception for an army which honestly believed itself to be marching to battle in an enemy's country.

The very evident fact was that the quick wits of the old capitalist parties had seen to the bottom of social reform within the existing order as soon as the advent of the Labour Party brought them face to face with the need for legislation on such lines. The Liberal Party, in particular, was fortunate in possessing, at the critical moment, men alert enough to see that the most effective way to safeguard the interests of the existing capitalist order was to meet the demands of the Labour Party ; and that a policy of social reform, in the most generous instalments, was not only consistent with the continued exploitation of labour by the master class, but was, in view of the demands of labour for such reform, in the interests of that exploitation ; a form of insurance to the exploiter class against attack on its main position, so long as the minds of the workers could be kept to by-paths within the existing order.

Hence it was that, in the very hour of its apparent Parliamentary success in securing large measures of such social reform, the Labour Party ceased to be any longer feared. The alarm with which its appearance in Parliament had been greeted died away, and its political opponents seldom missed an opportunity of declaring on their platforms their sense of how greatly Parliament had gained from the presence in it of these worthy and practical men representing the great working classes of this country. The tone of their private references to the Labour Party was somewhat less respectful than that of their platform utterances ; and showed, as anyone intimate with the private intercourse of politicians at that stage in the development of affairs will remember, that the capitalist parties believed they had fully taken the measure of the Labour representatives in the House of Commons, whom they regarded as a handful of easily flattered and easily managed futile men, trapped in the Parliamentary machine and overcome by their unaccustomed surroundings and position, pathetically insisting on the non-revolutionary character of their movement, and putting on the airs of that staid respectability and practical business capacity which their opponents daily assured them they possessed in so admirable a degree.

That was neither a fair nor a true estimate. There were, no doubt, certain superficial justifications for it, sufficient to make it current not only amongst the capitalist parties, but also amongst those of the rank and file of the Labour Party up and down the country who had some sort of understanding of the essentially revolutionary character of the economic change to which the formation of the Labour Party was only the political means. From that quarter there began to arise a steadily increasing complaint that the party was being betrayed by its Parliamentary representatives, who were constantly reminded that they were not sent to the House of Commons to be complimented by their opponents upon their political sagacity and practical statesmanship ; political sagacity and practical statesmanship being, from the point of view of the governing classes, any frame of mind which disturbed the existing order as little as possible.

This estimate of the Parliamentary representatives of the Labour Party was unfair and untrue, because it threw upon them the whole blame for inability to see beyond social reforms within the existing order. That they grievously under-estimated the force of revolutionary sentiment and synthetic economic thought in the movement must be admitted ; but the limitation of outlook attributed solely to them was really the limitation of the movement as a whole. They were honestly representing a movement which itself had not got beyond the empirical stage of pecking about like a hen at this detail and that detail of social reform within the existing order. It was the synthetic thinkers of the party who were as yet in a minority non-representative of the movement as a whole ; the working class consciousness behind the Parliamentary party had not yet attained to that. And those members of the Parliamentary group who did see pretty clearly what the economic development of their policy must ultimately be, and who discerned in a policy of social reform within the existing order the danger of the Labour Party losing its independent identity and becoming an auxiliary to whichever party took up such social reform most vigorously at the moment, had a good deal of force in their contention that the Labour movement could not be forced beyond its own economic conceptions, and that while it remained in the empirical stage in that respect, the most that its Parliamentary representatives could do was to keep alive the political class consciousness already attained by the workers, and trust to time and circumstances for the development of its economic vision.

What they overlooked in that calculation was the fact that, although the working classes might not yet have developed an economic class consciousness, there was still

K

going on that educational process of referring legislation back to the test of actual conditions in life and industry ; and that, in precisely the same way as governing class representation and Liberal-Labour representation had been judged by that test and found wanting, so, all over the country, the work and influence of the Labour Party in Parliament was being subjected to the same remorseless daily test. " Social reforms ?   There they are on paper and in the words of the statute book, no doubt.   But where are they in my home, in my wages, in my security of employment, in the raising of my standard of living ?   I cannot discover them there.   The feeding of necessitous school children is only evidence of the continued and untouched destitution of their parents in the actual conditions of industry.   And what I get in that way, in the prospect of getting from the Government at seventy the five shillings I should otherwise have got from the Poor Law, and from all your other social reforms put together, I have promptly lost in the increased prices of the necessaries of life."   So, looking at the daily facts of his life, the workman reasoned about the social reforms for which the Labour Party claimed that its influence had been mainly responsible.   A trifling change here and there, slight modifications in detail ; but all the great main features of poverty and of the essential relationship of the worker to society remaining untouched, unchanged ; the same old relationship of subjection and deprivation.

And so once again, from its perennial source in life and experience and the sting of daily felt injustice, the new impulse comes into the labour movement ; and at the very moment when the governing classes were congratulating themselves upon having very comfortably absorbed the Parliamentary Labour Party, there breaks out, with a dramatic completeness and an explosive vigour even more astonishing than that which characterized the first appearance of the Labour Party itself, this Labour Unrest everywhere.

Never, surely, had complacency and futility a more rude awakening. Everything was going on so prettily. The governing classes, having discovered that social reform within the existing order involved no hurt or loss to them, no interference with the exploitation of labour, no attack upon their mastery or diminution of their class privileges worth mentioning, were pleasantly engaged in voting social reforms on the one hand, and getting back in rents and prices what they were paying for it in rates and taxes on the other; under the comfortable delusion that because that sort of thimble-rig apparently satisfied the Parliamentary Labour Party, it would also serve to satisfy the working population behind the Labour Party. As for the Parliamentary Labour Party itself, its members, having recovered from their first surprise at finding themselves translated from the workshop and the trade union office to the most comfortable club in London, had settled down to the club life of the place as to the manner born, and were purring audibly at every compliment to the political sagacity which they showed by their continued and consistent support of the Government in office. The whole thing, after the scare of 1906 at the sudden emergence of Labour's political class consciousness, had settled down, so far as Westminster was concerned, into a beautiful quiescence.

And then, suddenly, this fierce eruption of discontent everywhere, shattering the complacency and the dream of peace!—the explosive violence and unmistakable emphasis of a living fact as against the political sagacity and paper statutes of the legislators; the entry of the real people of the drama upon the scene again, proclaiming, in a manner most jarring to the nerves of political sagacity, that they were still there, still hungry, still suffering deprivations and labouring under the sense of intolerable injustice to which political sagacity had as yet provided no adequate relief.

Always and insistently throughout the long struggle which we have now traced from its beginnings, it has come back to that, to the test of life and of daily experience. Always and insistently the proved futility of an achievement when brought to that test has been the beginning of new endeavour. But whereas, in the earlier stages, with the lack of education and the absence of a sense of working class solidarity, the reaction against a proved futility was often long drawn out, it is now prompt, widespread, and immediate on the heels of failure. There are to be no more delays spread over decades and generations. The insistence upon life, in a full human definition of it, is too urgent, too conscious of itself, too prompt in its realization of the failure of paper proposals to interpret themselves in daily experience, to permit such delay any more. Life is not to be fobbed off any longer on the pretence of waiting for a decade to see how this or that futility works out. The Labour Unrest is the social reform legislation of recent years returned to its authors with " Inadequate " written across it.

Its immediate effect upon political parties has been astonishing indeed, in view of the 1906 scare at the appearance of the Parliamentary Labour Party. Who would have dreamed, at that time, that within six years the Parliamentary Labour Party would itself be regarded as a safeguard for the old order against a new attack ? Truly the whirligig of Time brings about its revenges ; and the spectacle of a chairman of the Parliamentary Labour Party attending at the Board of Trade to secure the return of the railwaymen to work .without a scintilla of concession to their demands, and another one-time chairman stumping the country to secure the consent of the men to a Royal Commission Report, of which he and the employer representatives were joint signatories, a report in which the men saw no relief for their grievances, must be amongst the most unexpected of such revenges upon record. The capitalist interests of the country suddenly discovered that the root of the mischief was that the men disregarded their leaders, leaders known in Parliament for their political sagacity, their level-headedness, their practical qualities, leaders whom they were assured they ought to trust instead of breaking out in this undisciplined way. As for the leaders themselves, their amazement at the discovery that the Labour movement was something bigger and more closely related to actual life than the exhibition of political sagacity in Parliament found expression in scolding the working classes for indiscipline—a performance for which the only recorded precedent is that of the butterfly stamping its foot at King Solomon.

But life, the widespread life of the industrial classes, will not be denied its expression by the protests of politicians. It is the futility of the political accomplishment, its failure so far to effect any real change in conditions felt to be fundamentally unjust, that has produced this manifestation. And the unrest, so far from being settled, widens in area and grows in strength. It is the opening of the final phase in the struggle for complete democracy, evidence of the fact that life, with its insistence upon real attainment, has discovered the futility of political democracy by itself, and has started out to discover the economic synthesis which mates with the political synthesis already discerned and already found to be incomplete without its mate. A Labour Party without an economic synthesis of society, a Labour Party in the immature stage of economic empiricism, a non-revolutionary Labour Party devoted to social reform within the existing order, is seen to be only a passing phase in the approach of democracy to its real purposes and its inevitable maturity in economic equality.

The beginning of such a development is already manifest within the Parliamentary Labour Party itself.   From the outset it had included men whose growing uneasiness at the drift of the party into the position of jackal to the Government was open and undisguised, men with a sufficiently clear economic outlook to see that the policy being pursued would come to nothing, but hesitant about making a stand against it for fear of imperilling the existence of the party which they valued, and rightly valued, as the birth of the political class-consciousness of the workers, notwithstanding its economic blindness during what they hoped would be the very brief stage of its puppydom.   This little group within the party had kept itself as little as possible involved in the Government net, and the outbreak of the Labour Unrest was followed by their definite dissociation from the policy hitherto pursued by the party.   Their stand against the Insurance Act is the most significant indication, so far, of the Labour Party's certain advance out of empiricism to a rationale of economic democracy. And the pressure of the Labour Unrest for real conclusions, for attainments that hold good in life as well as upon paper, its prompt refusal to accept any solutions which still leave life squalid and without its full human satisfactions, may be trusted to secure that advance.

CHAPTER XI

INCREASED PRICES AND SOCIAL REFORM

THE immediate provoking cause of the Labour Unrest has been the all-round increase in the cost of living, and its most striking characteristic has been that it is directed to no definite immediate end.

The general public has become accustomed in the past to strikes and labour disputes for resisting some definite new condition sought to be imposed by employers upon workmen in respect of wages, hours of labour, or the like, or for insisting upon some definite advance of a like nature. But the difficulty about the Labour Unrest has been to discern any such definite objective in it. In very many cases, the men seem hardly to have known what they were out for in any clearly defined way. It is, as is indicated by the very name which has been instinctively applied to it, an unrest, a general ferment, a vague universal discontent expressing itself in protest, not against this or that clearly-defined detail of injustice, but against the general condition in which working-men have to live.

It is not the less, but infinitely the more significant for that. A definite strike for a definite purpose in a definite industry or locality is a trifling thing compared with this. Such strikes are undertaken by men whose view of their human destiny may be confined within the narrowest limits of the existing order, seeking a little easement of the saddle on this or that sore, but accepting it without question as their fate and the fate of their class to be ridden for all time. But the present Labour Unrest is a true revolutionary ferment, the pressure of human life against the limitations set for it by the existing order. Inarticulate as it is, the thought which it is struggling to express is discernible enough to any one who will apply the mind's ear to its indistinctness of utterance. " Here are two ways of living in this world of abundant resources ; the one spacious, the other poor ; the one distinctive of ownership, the other distinctive of labour and wage-earning. And we who are wage-earners find the poor way unsatisfying, no longer tolerable.''

The how and the why of it may not be as yet fully articulate, but the nature of the Labour Unrest as a demand by human life upon the resources of the world for human satisfactions from which it has hitherto been shut out, is clear as a bell striking the hour. It is a demand directed against the social order within which such satisfactions are denied, against class distinctions in the enjoyment of the human heritage of life in its fullest human definition ; a demand inevitably bound to come, sooner or later, with the spread of intelligence and of political power amongst the disinherited class ; a demand that will not cease until the how and the why are known and the way found.

It comes from men who thought they had found a way when they attained their political class-consciousness, and sent their men to Parliament to accelerate the pace of social reform within the existing order ; and it is the cry of their disillusionment on finding, by the daily experience of life, that the ends they had hoped to attain are not being attained, and are not in the least likely to be attained, in that way. And the immediate provoking cause of their disillusionment has been the all-round increase in the cost of living following promptly upon the attainment of social reforms within the existing order.

It was upon that rock of increasing rents and prices that the whole delusion of the possibility of effective social reform within the existing order was bound from the outset to come to exposure and wreck. The process by which the master class can, so long as they are left in possession of the sources of wealth, get back with one hand what they are compelled to give with the other, became an open and avowed process when, in the course of the negotiations for a settlement of the railway dispute, the Government took it for granted that powers must, of course, be given to the railway companies to raise rates and charges to whatever extent might be necessary to make up for increased wages or the cost of improved conditions. And what held good, in that quite open and avowed way, in the case of the railway companies—in whose case it was necessary openly to declare it only because the railway companies differ from most other capitalist undertakings in having their charges subject to some degree of control by legislation and the Board of Trade—holds good equally throughout the whole range of industrial life. When the coal-miners get an advance of wages, coal prices go up to cover the amount of the advance, and generally a margin more. The miners do not get their advance from their masters, but by a decrease in the purchasing power of the wages of all workers throughout the country in respect of one of the necessaries of life. And so it is all round. The general level of profits taken by the master class is not affected by these concessions, the cost of which is passed on to the consumer, and falls ultimately upon wages in the form of decreased purchasing power. Given an equal, simultaneous, all-round rise in wages in all industries, and the position of the workers would be as it was before. They would each be paying in increased prices for the increase in wages of all the others. They might call their wages twenty-five shillings instead of a pound, but the twenty-five shillings would only give them the same purchasing power, the same supply of the necessaries of life, as the pound did.

And if that is so—as daily experience shows it to be—with direct increases of wages or changes in the conditions of employment raising the cost of production and the nominal price of labour as a commodity in the market, it is equally so with levies made in other ways upon the profits and incomes of the master class. These levies are promptly passed on. The whole of the Liberal case against Tariff Reform is based upon a recognition of this fact. The consumer pays. " Your food will cost you more.

By precisely the same reasoning, and in precisely the same way, the whole of the cost of social reform levied by taxation upon profits and unearned incomes is passed on, and reflects itself in a generally increased cost of the commodities and the services from which the profits and the incomes are drawn. Leave the proprietary class in possession of the sources of wealth, and they can automatically recoup themselves for any such charges you choose to put upon them.

It is in the very nature of private capitalism that this should happen. Private ownership of the sources of wealth exists for the fulfilment of a perfectly clear and definite function— the function of levying tribute upon industry. And it will continue to function so long as it exists ; and, while it functions, the national resources will not be available for the national life, because the very nature of its function is to divert those resources out of the national life into the possession of the owners of our sources of wealth. Given private ownership of the sources of the national wealth, and the process is as inevitable as gravitation.

The simple-minded person, therefore, who thinks that by getting social reform within the existing order—that is, social reform which leaves private capitalism in possession of the sources of wealth—he can get an appreciably larger proportion of the resources of the nation into the lives of the workers, is asking private capitalism to abrogate the very law of its existence. That certain minor collateral advantages may be attained that way is not questioned. It is an advantage, for example, to get the regular assurance which an old age pension at seventy gives, as against the uncertainty and scramble of dependence upon one's private chances. But the notion that all these reforms in any way affect the broad general distribution of the wealth of the country between narrow subsistence for labour on the one hand and all the surplus over and above that narrow subsistence for ownership on the other hand, is a notion to which daily experience is now giving the lie in the clearest possible fashion. The general all-round increase in the cost of the necessaries of life and the expense of keeping a working-class home going is simply the propertied classes recouping themselves, by increased rents and charges and prices, for the levies made upon them for the social reforms of recent years. The workman is paying in this way for his own social reform, and is on the whole no better off than before. Life is teaching him the inexorable lesson that

private capitalism will continue to function so
long as it remains private capitalism, owning
the means of his work and the sources of the
national wealth, and that he cannot get round
that fact along the by-path of social reform.

The essential injustice—the relationship of
the worker to society as a commodity, the
fundamental fact of disinheritance—remains
absolutely untouched by all this. In the
development of their political class-consciousness the workers had already so far developed
their economic class-consciousness as to grasp
the primary fact that the power of one man
over another man's subsistence, the rule
of one man over another man's employment,
is just as much an attack upon life as the power
of inflicting physical injury with a bludgeon ;
that the right to discharge a man into unemployment and hunger is identical, in its attack
upon life, with the power to knife him ;
and that livelihood held subject to that right
is not the livelihood of free men. They began
the exercise of their political power with
the hope of meeting this attack, the vague
and indeterminate hope of somehow or other
nullifying it by social reform ; vague and
indeterminate because it was the hope of
men who, though they felt their injuries, had
as yet no clear knowledge of how those injuries

L

were inflicted, not by the excesses of private capitalism, but by the very nature of the industrial organization of society. To that clear knowledge they had to come by the old road, the only road, the road of experience. And their first experience of social reform upon a wholesale scale within the existing order was sufficient to show them that here was no likelihood of warding off the injuries inflicted upon them. At its very best and in its completion—assuming it to be carried to the farthest point—all this, they began to see, was merely ambulance legislation, a picking up of the wounded and injured which in itself was evidence of the continuance of the attack upon life. Old-age pensions were only an indication of the fact that the industrial organization of society was such as to leave old age destitute and stricken ; mere ambulance work, rendered necessary by the ruthlessness with which the assault upon life was still being carried on. The feeding of necessitous school children was only a sort of concentration camp provision, rendered necessary because the homes of their parents were still being remorselessly stripped of resources. The whole business of social reform on ambulance lines assumed and took for granted the continued existence of social injustice, the continued infliction of the injuries for which these crutches and bandages were required. Not one step was it all leading towards a settlement, or even a discernment, of that primary injustice.

So reasoned the wage-earner, driven back by the inexorable logic of events upon the primary facts of life. Once again, as so often throughout the long struggle, he brought his supposed attainment to the test of daily experience, and found it wanting ; found it nothing but an inflated form of the charity and philanthropy with which sympathetic people have always tried to alleviate suffering without realizing that all such charity and philanthropy is evidence of defective social organization, and that the more there is occasion for it, the worse is the indictment against the social system in which it is needed.

Legislation on such ambulance lines is, of course, not without its beneficial results. Assuming that it is hopeless to attempt to stop the attack upon life, the organization of a National Crutch and Bandage Department on the most generous possible scale is a very desirable thing. The mistake is in supposing it to be the emancipation of labour, or even a step in that direction, the beginning of an

organization of the industrial affairs of the
nation upon a footing of justice. That was
the mistake which the Parliamentary Labour
Party were making ; and it is against that
delusion that the Labour Unrest breaks in
wave after wave, a rising tide of general and
continued discontent with and revolt against
the conditions of working class life.

And it is beginning to be discerned that,
while the Labour Party has to a large extent,
sufficient extent to dominate its Parliamentary
action, remained under the influence of that
delusion, the capitalist parties have seen
through it quite clearly ; and are now devot-
ing themselves to this ambulance legislation
of social reform within the existing order for
the express and avowed purpose of warding
off the democratic attack upon the main
injustice. They have accepted the ambulance
analogy quite frankly. " I ask the House,"
said Mr. Winston Churchill, on the second
reading of the Trade Boards Bill, " to regard
these sweated industries as sick and diseased
industries. I ask Parliament to deal with
them exactly in the same mood and temper
as we should deal with sick people. It would
be absurd to apply to the healthy the restrictions required for the sick. Let the House
think of these sweated trades as patients in

a hospital ward. Each case must be studied and treated entirely by itself. No general rule can be applied. Different medicines, different diets, different operations are required for each ; and consideration, encouragement, nursing, personal effort are necessary for all." And again, in his book on " Liberalism and the Social Problem," he says :—" We want to draw a line below which we will not allow persons to live and labour, yet above which they may compete with all the strength of their manhood. . . . The main body of the army has won its victory. It has moved out into the open plain, into a pleasant camping-ground by the water springs, and in the sunshine, amid fair cities and fertile fields. But the rearguard is entangled in the defiles, the rearguard is still struggling in mountainous country, encumbered with wounded, obstructed by all the broken vehicles that have fallen back from the main line of the march, with all the stragglers and weaklings that have fallen by the way."

The purpose of the capitalist parties in promoting social reform within the existing order is here clearly defined. It is to preserve vested interests by trimming them of some of their worst excesses, and by making provision for dealing in hospital fashion with the broken and wounded lives that litter the field of their operations. So far from ending the essential injustice of the worker's normal status of disinheritance, his position in society as a commodity fighting for its price, social reform as promoted by the capitalist parties assumes that the worker is to continue to struggle in that position "with all the strength of his manhood," and that if only an adequate hospital provision is set up for the injured, labour may be persuaded to regard its normal position as "a pleasant camping ground by the water springs, and in the sunshine, amid fair cities and fertile fields," and abandon any idea of such fundamental change as involves attack upon vested interests in their essential injustice.

The Labour Unrest is the grim and scoffing laughter of human nature at that rhetorical picture of what constitutes adequate satisfaction for human life. For it is not an unrest amongst "the rearguard struggling in the defiles." It is the unrest of the main body of the working population, regularly employed and under the normal conditions of industrial life, in their "pleasant camping ground by the water springs and in the sunshine, amid fair cities and fertile fields"; proclaiming that the water springs are bitter and the sunshine darkened by injustice, and that all the perorations of all the frothy rhetoricians in the service of the master class cannot make " fair cities and fertile fields " out of the hell of modern civilization, as the wage-earner experiences it in his daily life.

Social reform within the existing order is deliberately intended to buttress the social system which prescribes for the wage-earner the economic status of a commodity, and to protect the class interests which are dependent upon the continuance of that relationship of the worker to society. Its purpose, more and more openly avowed, is to produce a servile contentment with that status, and with the industrial order based upon it, by assuring to the worker some degree of medical attention for his injuries received in it, and some minimum of security against the more extreme consequences of regulating society upon such a footing at all.

The indictment which Mr. Hilaire Belloc has brought against the Parliamentary Labour Party for being diverted out of the revolutionary road into support of this capitalist policy of social reform within the existing order—the indictment that all this, if it should succeed in imposing upon the mind of the worker and be carried to its furthest expression, would lead, not to emancipation, but to the Servile State—is unanswerable. He .defines the Servile State thus :—" You recognize, or if necessary you impose, a state of society in which the mass of your inhabitants—I won't say your citizens—are permanently dispossessed of the means of production.   You differentiate the community into two classes, those who possess the means of production and those who do not.   But you get security and sufficiency for all by organization.   You see to it, if you are humane, that the man who is not in possession of the means of production shall not be oppressed and that the punishments that will compel him to work are moderate and not excessive.   You see to it that he lives the life which happens to suit your own particular ideal of the minimum of human comfort, but you do not put the means of production into his hands, either directly or indirectly.   He is a slave.   Whether you use the word or whether you do not, that acceptation of one class permanently in possession of the means of production, and another side by side with it permanently dispossessed of the same, is what makes the Servile State, and that is what makes the slave class.   And the other people, who own the means of production, you conversely, by the very act of creating a slave class, confirm in their possession of the means of production. You make them stronger in their citadel than before. You may prevent their being cruel; you may prevent everything which you do not like on the fringes of their action; but you do not take away their capital, and you do not take away their land."

That is the Servile State, which it is the deliberate purpose of social reform within the existing order to build up as a strong security and citadel for private ownership of the sources of wealth. Mr. Belloc, who hates it violently, nevertheless falls into the same error as do the capitalist parties who devoutly believe in it, in assuming that because the Parliamentary Labour Party has for the moment been entrapped into joining in this capitalist adventure, the general working class population will also be imposed upon by it; and that it will be possible to get a nation of workers content with improvements in their condition within the limits of their continued servile status in society.

That calculation leaves human nature out of account. It assumes that thought will cease. It overlooks the fact that the class

which it supposes can be kept in a permanently servile status by having buttered crusts
thrown to it, and a little more straw put into
its mattress, is a class in the possession of
political power and of intelligence. Given
human nature under those conditions, the
spread of intelligence and the growth of a
consciousness of political power ; and no
permanent servile status is thinkable for it.
So far from producing contentment with the
existing order, every little increased margin
to life means more opportunity for the spread
of intelligence, and consequently more discontent with the existing order itself.

The Labour Unrest is a final and convincing
proof of that.   Those who either fear like Mr.
Belloc, or hope, like the capitalist parties in
politics, for a Servile State as a citadel for
class privilege to come of social reform within
the existing order, would do well to note the
fact that it is precisely amongst the better
class artisans that the unrest expresses itself
most clearly in revolutionary terms.   Amongst
the people in the worst slums, in the most
sweated industries, in the world of underpaid
rural labour, there is as yet very little
Socialism.   These people are either hopeless
in their despair, sunk into animalism and a
scramble for whatever charity may be going,

or most easily hoodwinked into believing this or that trifling detail of social reform will give them all they can conceive of human beings as requiring for the satisfaction of life. It is amongst the better-paid, better-conditioned artisans that the synthetic conception of Socialism as a new order of society, challenging the very class foundation of the existing order, has taken hold most vigorously and carried the mind of the worker out and beyond the peddling futilities of social reform. The Servile State might be possible if you kept your servile class uneducated and without political rights. But to educate men, to give them access to the literature and philosophy and science of the world, and to place them in possession of political power ; and then to expect them to remain content with a status of dispossession tempered by hospitals and ambulances, is to misinterpret human nature in the most ridiculous way.

The fact that the Parliamentary Labour Party has been out-manœuvred for the moment matters little or nothing. It is not as though its errors were the errors of a mature party deliberately deviating from a clearly seen purpose of emancipation into a betrayal of its cause. Nothing of the sort has happened. Its errors have been the errors of experiment

and of half-seen purpose natural to a newly-
born party suddenly thrust into an environment remotely alien from all its knowledge of
life ; called upon to act in that environment
without experience, and subject to the steady
daily influence, pressure, and intrigue against
it of astute politicians of the older parties
to whom the art of managing Parliament had
been a study for generations.   The new men
were   made   extremely   comfortable.   They
were listened to with respect, and every device
of flattery was brought to bear upon the task
of assimilating them to House of Commons'
ways   and   traditions   of   procedure.   They
were led by insensible daily pressure and
association to feel that the men they met
there, the astute representatives of the
governing order, were not such bad fellows
after all, and that on the whole it would be
bad form to say to their faces in the House the
sort of thing that used to be good enough for
the trade union club room or the Labour
meeting outside.   It was difficult to keep that
sort of thing up with men with whom you
spent long hours in the smoke room, men
whom you were coming insensibly to regard
as affable fellow-clubmen.   The whole atmosphere of the place made for comfort and
quiescence, for the avoidance of the revolu-

tionary note. And those one or two men in the party who showed a real zest for the Parliamentary game, and some promise of becoming masters of it, were specially selected for flattery, not only in the House, but in all the capitalist newspapers. Their political sagacity was contrasted with the bitterness into which some of their less easily assimilated colleagues occasionally broke out. They were constantly assured of the high intellectual respect in which the House held them ; and every subtle influence at the command of the governing-class parties was brought to bear upon them. Was it any wonder that the Labour movement became more and more to them simply this game of a career spent in Parliamentary futilities, that the impact of the living movement outside reached them through constantly thickening layers of Parliamentary cotton wool, and that they should under-estimate the strength of that growing revolutionary purpose in the movement which they felt instinctively to be uncongenial to the tone of the House, and death to the repute for political sagacity of any man who voiced it there ? They had come there without any definite economic mandate beyond social reform within the existing order. They were organized for no clearly defined purpose of industrial emancipation. Their commission had been made out only in terms of a vague desire for betterment. And the marvel is, not that they were influenced in this way by their Parliamentary environment, but that under such conditions they withstood it so much as they did ; preserving intact their party, as an expression of the independent political class consciousness of the wage-earners, against the most serious danger which could possibly have threatened its infant existence ; the danger of having its policy of social betterment appropriated and carried out by the older parties in such a way as to compel the Labour men to figure constantly in the public eye as supporters and auxiliaries of the Government.

The Labour Unrest brings that dangerous period of infancy to a close. It tears up the old commission, the old mandate for vague social betterment, and begins to write out a new commission in bolder terms, terms of a more clearly seen economic purpose, dealing with the essential relationship of the worker to society ; and therefore not capable of being confused with the commission of any capitalist party, because its fulfilment means the real attack upon class privilege.

The old commission has been discovered

to be practically worthless ; and the terms of the new commission, readable in clearer and clearer definition with every day that passes, are that nothing really matters except getting the sources of wealth out of the hands of a class, and into the possession of the whole nation.

CHAPTER XII

THAT is the new synthetic conception of the economic relationship of the worker to society to which the whole movement for social betterment is now visibly shaping. Face to face with that clearly seen purpose the long struggle of a century towards the emancipation of labour from inferior conditions of life was bound to bring us in the end. The driving force, the constant urge and importunity of human life against deprivations, has been incessant throughout the whole process. Beginning as a vague and indeterminate resentment of what it felt to be the injustice of its lot in life, it was destined, by the inherent qualities of the human mind, which is a living intelligence and not a machine, to arrive sooner or later at a clear definition of that injustice ; and equally bound, by the limitations of the human mind, to arrive at that definition only after a long process of experiment, of half-seen purposes ; steadily eliminating error and growing more comprehensive in its calculations towards the final and effective synthesis.

We have followed this struggle of human life against its deprivations through all its phases and its constant enlargement. Trade unionism, political rights, the Labour Party and social reform within the existing order—with each enlargement of its campaign the Labour movement has come back again and again to the primary evil untouched, the essential injustice still there ; and the attainment of satisfying conditions of life always thwarted by some ungrasped factor in the problem so far not taken into account. Deeper and wider as the operations of Labour in this campaign have been carried on, something has obviously been taken for granted, some fundamental thing allowed to remain unchallenged, in all that has been done so far ; so fundamental as to nullify every attainment which fails to take it into account and include it in the challenge.

This fundamental thing has at last been discerned to be the private ownership of the sources of wealth.

Nothing really matters so long as that remains. The essential human purpose of all the movement and unrest of the last

M

hundred years has been to make the resources of the nation available for the life of the nation, and that purpose remains unattained and unattainable so long as the sources of wealth are owned and controlled by a master class. Make what regulations you please against the cruelty and extremity to which their mastery may be carried ; the fact of their mastery over human life, inherent in their mastery over the means of human life, remains ; the disinheritance of the worker and his relationship to society as a mere commodity remains ; the broad fact remains of a subsistence price for that commodity in the market, and the diversion of all the resources of the nation, over and above that subsistence, into the possession of the master class by virtue of their mastery over the sources of wealth.

While society continues to be organized on that foundation of private ownership of the sources of wealth, the private owners, and the private owners alone, are to all intents and purposes the nation ; and the rest of us are only here on sufferance for their profit and convenience. They are the lords of men by virtue of their lordship of the means by which men must live. Nobody outside the charmed circle of ownership has any

status except the status of a commodity
which may or may not be wanted by the
owners, nor any interest in wealth production
other than the interest of hawking in the labour
market his capacity for producing wealth for
an owner, and selling that commodity for
permission to retain subsistence out of what
he produces. He is purchased or not purchased according to the prospect which the
owner sees of his producing wealth beyond
the cost of his subsistence; and he has no
place or status in the nation except on being
so purchased. That is his relationship to
society, a relationship which he can never
alter except by securing access in his own
right as a man and a citizen to the means of
his work.

Here, upon a square mile of earth, live a
hundred men, a human community, born into
the world, one to the ownership of the land
upon which they all must live, the others
non-owners. What is the exact nature of
the one man's ownership? Is it not obvious
that it is not merely ownership of land, but
ownership of the other men? For the land
is the source of their wealth, the means by
which they live. Their general labour can
make it fruitful; from it they must draw their
sustenance. And the man who can say of

the land, " It is mine," can say of the men,
" They are mine." He is the community.
They can only get their sustenance by his
permission. Their status is that of a commodity, labour, which he purchases by permitting it to work, and, having worked, to
retain, as wages, a portion of the value of its
product. Everything they produce is his, for
the land is his. Their opportunity of main-
taining themselves by their labour is only
given to them on condition of their main-
taining him also ; the total sustenance drawn
from the land being allocated in bare sustenance for them and all the surplus for him—
the cottage way of life and the mansion way
of life ; the robbery of labour made possible
by the ownership of the common source of
the community's wealth.

And what is true, very obviously true, in
the simple primitive relationship of land and
labour is equally true throughout the whole
intricate range of wealth production. The
intricacy is only a multiplication of details,
and does not in the least affect the nature of
the relationship between industry and ownership of the sources of the world's wealth.
The distribution of wealth for use and con-
sumption is governed by the ownership of its
sources.

That fact of private ownership defines the existing industrial order. Progress towards making the national resources available for the national life is impossible within that order ; because the very purpose of ownership, the reason for its existence, is to secure the national resources as tribute to ownership. You can only make progress within it as a squirrel makes progress in a turning-cage. Higher wages, or levies by taxation upon the tribute taken by ownership, give way under your feet as a step up a treadmill gives way, and the increased cost of living brings you to the same level as before.

It has taken us a hundred years to learn the simple lesson that the nation must own and control the sources of its wealth, holding them for the general benefit of all, if it is to make its resources available for the general national life. Notwithstanding all our social reform legislation, the real rulers of the nation, the owners of land, of coal, of railways, of iron, the real rulers by virtue of their ownership of the means of life, have gone on governing in actual life, carrying on the national industry for their private profit and and interest ; and the whole industrial system has functioned for their profit, as it will inevitably continue to function so long as they retain their rule by holding the sources of wealth.

The reasons for our long delay in arriving at an understanding of a principle which, when once clearly stated, is so self-evident, so complete in its interpretation of the facts of life, are twofold. First, the enormous difficulty of getting the average man to question an established order of things. It escapes scrutiny because it is the established order, which everybody takes for granted as being part of the permanent foundation matter of the world. That has been the frame of mind of most people about private landownership and private mastery over the means of industry. It no more occurred to the average man to question these things than to question the rising and setting of the sun ; and not till ingenuity had been exhausted in the attempt to explain the poverty of the workers amidst abundant wealth in every conceivable way within the existing order was it likely that the existing order itself should come under question and scrutiny as the possible cause of all the trouble.

And, in the second place, delay was inevitable until the political, as distinct from the economic, philosophy of democracy had been sufficiently realized to enable men to conceive of the State as the whole nation acting in co-operation. At the beginning of the nineteenth century the State was not the nation, but only the governing classes. The people had no political rights. Hence, had it occurred to any one that the root of industrial poverty was in the separation between the worker and the means of his work, national ownership would not have seemed a way out of the difficulty ; because national ownership would still have meant class government of industry. And since, in the very nature of the new modern machine tools of production, they were incapable of being individually handled, and the worker could not therefore be brought into direct access to the means of his work by individual ownership, there appeared to be no way out of the existing order. Before the idea of national ownership of the sources of wealth could present itself to the mind of the worker as the attainment of his own mastery, in co-operation with his fellows, over the conditions of his industrial life, it was necessary that the political revolution should have transformed the State from a class coterie into the self-governing nation. The worker had to realize himself in political citizenship before he could realize himself in economic and industrial citizenship ; and until the political process had been carried sufficiently far to give its new democratic definition to the State, the worker had no reason to look for any emancipating quality in State organization of industry and ownership of the sources of wealth.

The time spent upon the conquest of political power was, therefore, by no means wasted. It was the necessary preliminary to the realization of economic freedom through citizenship.

Meanwhile the area of discontent with the existing order widens rapidly. What was the middle class thirty or forty years ago has now gone largely to recruit the ranks of the disinherited. The development of the great joint-stock company has made it increasingly difficult for the small independent capitalist to hold his own. The small shopkeeper, the small factory owner," the little man in a small but comfortable way of business," is being hustled out of existence. Capital tends to greater and greater aggregations. The joint-stock company itself becomes absorbed in the still greater trust and syndicate. The ousted middle class is supplying the disinherited class with regiments of an intellectual proletariat, fiercely discontented ; their old security gone, and at best only some upper servant's place available for them under the newer developments of plutocracy.

Yet another and remarkable strengthening of the forces making for national ownership as the only solution of these industrial troubles has been very evident during the past two years. So far we have considered the Labour Unrest, and the long movement leading up to and explaining it, only from the point of view of working-class life struggling for its human recognition and status in the nation, against the deprivations inflicted upon it by our present industrial system. But every incident in the Labour Unrest, every stoppage of work and period of public inconvenience, has helped to rouse the nation as a whole, in its capacity as a nation of consumers, to the absurdity of private ownership. When, recently, the railway service of the nation was dislocated and business thrown into general confusion, the exquisite absurdity of permitting our railway system, a thing essential to the convenience of the whole nation, to be regarded as the private business of a handful of practically uncontrolled railway directors, became clearly manifest to thousands upon thousands of people to whom the idea of railway nationalization had never before seriously occurred. The whole nation was told, in effect, to mind its own business, and that this was not its business. It was the business of the railway companies, and if they chose to carry on a private war with their men, the general public must stand quietly on one side and suffer the inconvenience of it until such time as it pleased the railway companies and their men to come to terms.

The general public, through that experience, realized amongst other things that the railway system of the country is primarily and essentially the country's business. And every incident in the Labour Unrest, just in proportion to the degree of inconvenience which it has inflicted upon the public, has taught the same lesson. The nation has begun to reason with itself on the matter, and to look for object lessons. A strong navy, it argues, is a national necessity; and because it is a primary national necessity we maintain and equip it. But coal is equally a national necessity. Why should we not own and control our coal supply as we own and control our navy, organizing the getting of coal and its distribution throughout the nation at a standard price as a branch of the national service? Why not railways on the same footing? And why not, generally, the production and distribution of our resources as

public services carried on for national use ?
Is it not rather mad of us to permit coal,
which we must have, to become a private
kingdom, ruled over by a private government
drawing vast revenues out of us by private
taxation ?   For are not its profits a form of
taxation ?   The natural price of a commodity
is the cost of its production.   The coal kings
charge us prices far in excess of that.   What is
that excess but taxation levied for the upkeep
of this private government ?   Why should we
be grandmothered in that expensive way
instead of organizing our own national supplies for our own use and service ?

The Labour Unrest has brought this aspect
of the matter very forcibly home to the public
mind ;   and this new and rapidly growing
public opinion, under the constant incitement
of being told that its own convenience in
respect of services and supplies essential to its
daily life is not its business at all, but the
business of the private kings who rule over
those services and supplies, regulating their
conduct solely from the point of view of getting in the largest possible amount of revenue
from their kingdoms by the double process of
making the cost of labour as little as possible
and the charge for supplies to the consumer
as much as possible, this rapidly growing

public opinion is being linked up with the discontent of Labour in making the new synthesis of national organization of industry a practical possibility. For Labour and the consumer stand in essentially the same relationship to the rulers over the means of life. Neither of them exists for their own human ends and convenience, but only to provide revenue for the private governments in industry. Labour provides that revenue by being a commodity to be purchased as cheaply as possible, and, when purchased, producing more than what it can be bought for. The consumer provides revenue by having to pay, in addition to the cost of producing the things he needs, the largest possible amount he can be got to pay rather than go without them. The whole industrial system, first and last and through and through, is organized for the levy of this tribute upon the community.

And against that maniac way of conducting the affairs of civilized people there now arises the synthetic idea of the nation organizing its own services for its own use and enjoyment, owning and working the sources of its own wealth, and freeing itself from the tribute which now strips it for the profit of these private lordships ; a co-operative commonwealth in which the worker and the consumer and the owner shall be the same person, the citizen who is owner by the inherent right of his citizenship, and consumer only by his right as a worker rendering service to the commonwealth. So, and so only, can the national resources be made available for the general national life : by the working out of the economic implications of democracy; government by the people for the people of the people in respect of industry as well as in respect of political enfranchisement.

The structural weakness of the existing social order in face of the democratic idea is self-evident. With the masses of the people educated and in possession of political power, a social organization which does not produce economic equality and work to a general standard of common well-being is a social organization in a condition of unstable equilibrium.

The Labour Unrest exhibits such a social organization in its final stage of top-heaviness, reeling over by the pressure of human life against the deprivations which it necessarily imposes upon the mass of men. Necessarily imposes, because a mass of propertyless men in the labour market is an essential condition of capitalist production ; and the continued existence of a mass of propertyless men is

no longer a permanent possibility once education and political power become widespread
amongst them. No longer a possibility, no
longer even thinkable. Whoever believes a
stable order of society to be possible upon a
basis of educated and politically powerful
human lives deprived of their full human
satisfactions, is a fool and blind.

JARROLD & SONS, WARWICK LANE, LONDON, E.C.

Printed in Great Britain
by Amazon